GRAPHIC LIBRARY™

NANCY WAKE
Fearless Spy of WORLD WAR II

by Jessica Gunderson

illustrated by Alice Larsson

CAPSTONE PRESS
a capstone imprint

Published by Capstone Press, an imprint of Capstone.
1710 Roe Crest Drive, North Mankato, Minnesota 56003
capstonepub.com

Library of Congress Cataloging-in-Publication Data is available on the
Library of Congress website
ISBN: 9781666334128 (hardcover)
ISBN: 9781666334135 (paperback)
ISBN: 9781666334142 (ebook PDF)

Summary: In the early 1940s, during World War II, Germany's Nazi regime
expanded into neighboring European countries. In France, groups of anti-
Nazi citizens, known as the French Resistance, fought to stop Germany's
reign of terror. A brave woman named Nancy Wake became one of the
movement's greatest assets as a spy. In her role, Wake often transported
Jewish people to safe locations and rode her bicycle through German
checkpoints to deliver messages and supplies. For her ability to avoid
capture, the enemy nicknamed her the "White Mouse."

Editorial Credits
Editor: Donald Lemke; Designer: Tracy Davies;
Production Specialist: Katy LaVigne

Design Elements: Shutterstock/Here

All internet sites appearing in back matter were available and accurate
when this book was sent to press.

Printed and bound in the USA. 4882

TABLE OF CONTENTS

IF I HAVE THE CHANCE

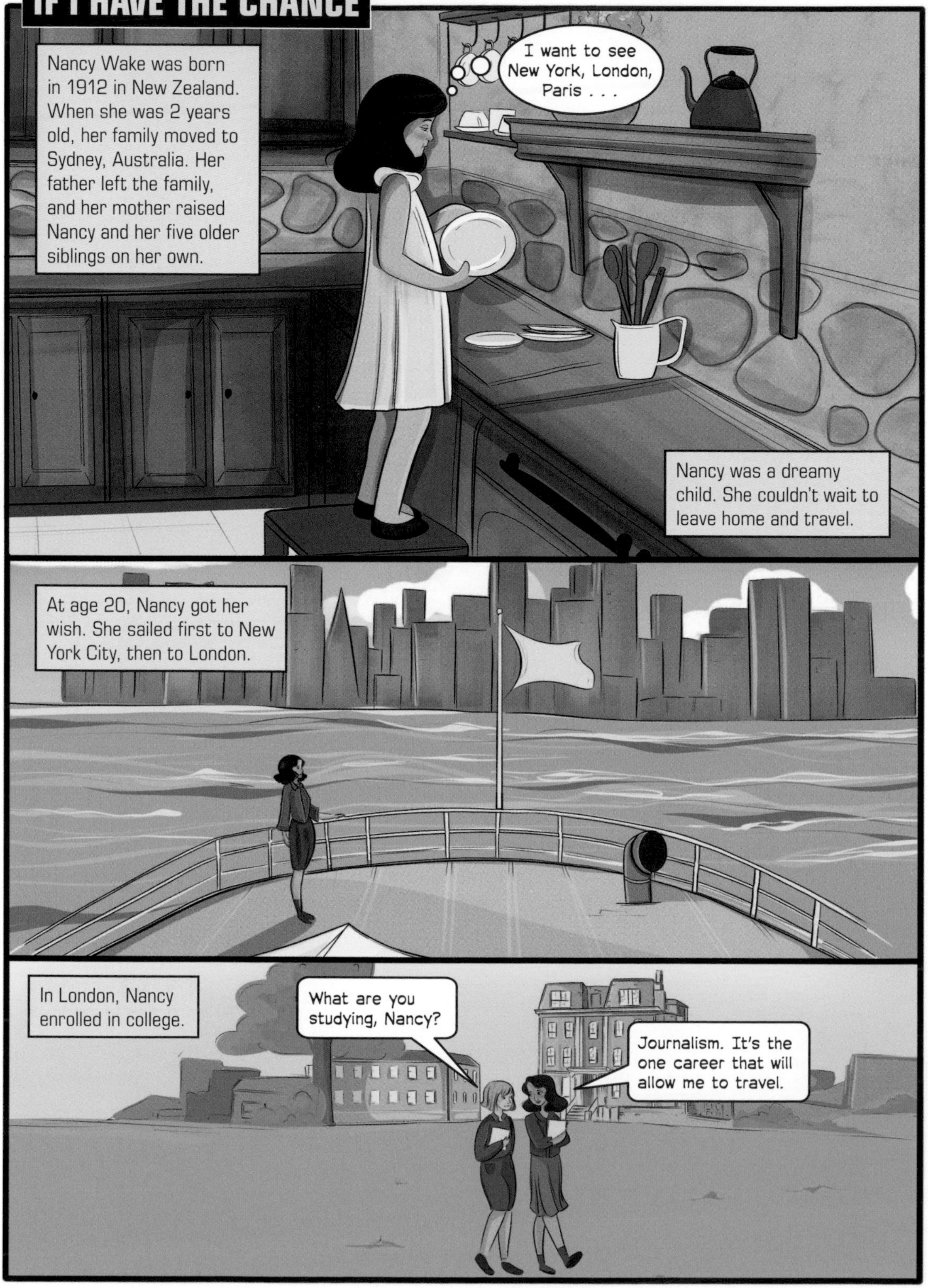
Nancy Wake was born in 1912 in New Zealand. When she was 2 years old, her family moved to Sydney, Australia. Her father left the family, and her mother raised Nancy and her five older siblings on her own.
I want to see New York, London, Paris . . .
Nancy was a dreamy child. She couldn't wait to leave home and travel.
At age 20, Nancy got her wish. She sailed first to New York City, then to London.
In London, Nancy enrolled in college.
What are you studying, Nancy?
Journalism. It's the one career that will allow me to travel.

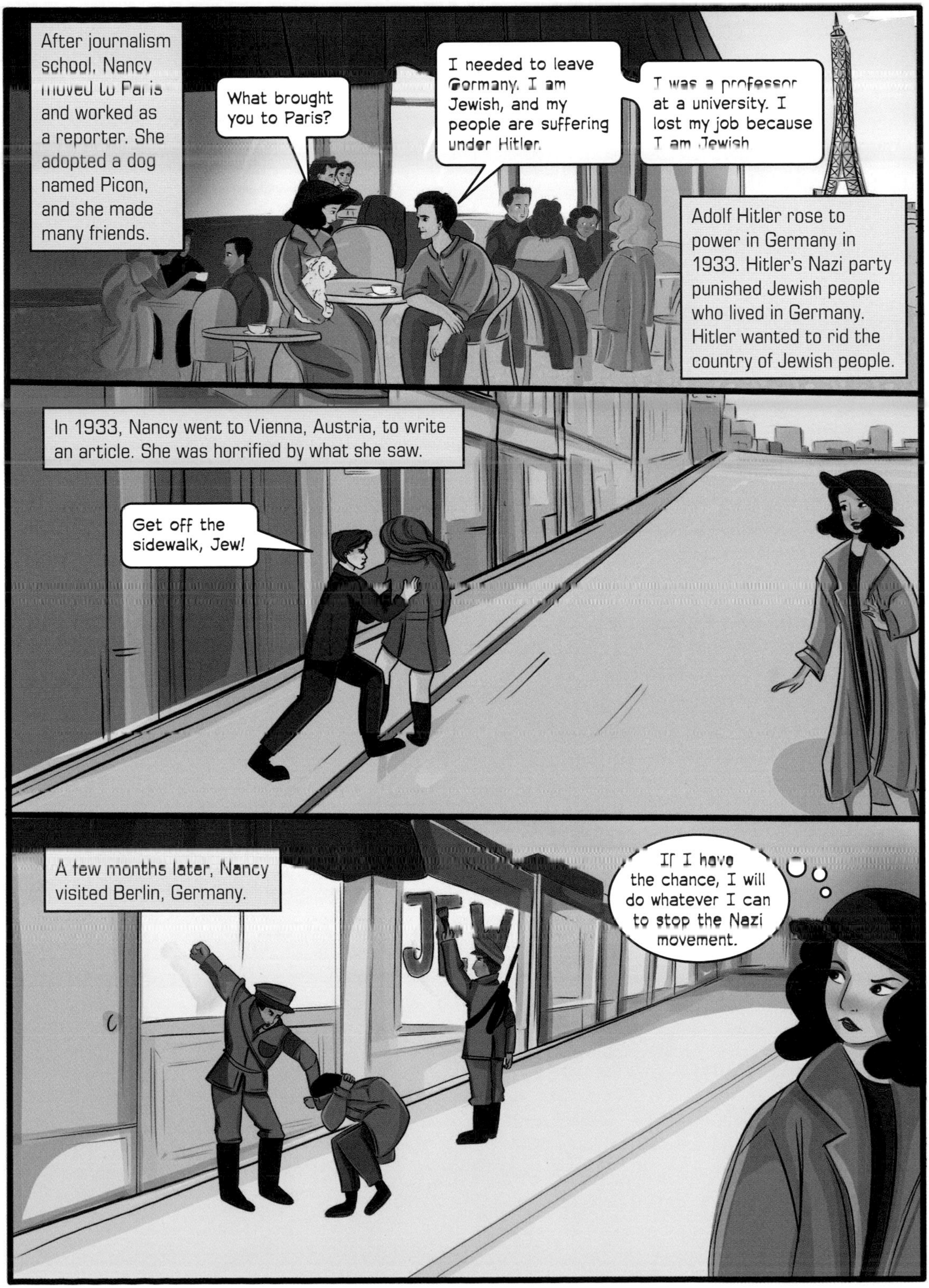

After journalism school, Nancy moved to Paris and worked as a reporter. She adopted a dog named Picon, and she made many friends.
What brought you to Paris?
I needed to leave Germany. I am Jewish, and my people are suffering under Hitler.
I was a professor at a university. I lost my job because I am Jewish.
Adolf Hitler rose to power in Germany in 1933. Hitler's Nazi party punished Jewish people who lived in Germany. Hitler wanted to rid the country of Jewish people.
In 1933, Nancy went to Vienna, Austria, to write an article. She was horrified by what she saw.
Get off the sidewalk, Jew!
A few months later, Nancy visited Berlin, Germany.
JEW
If I have the chance, I will do whatever I can to stop the Nazi movement.

THE WHITE MOUSE

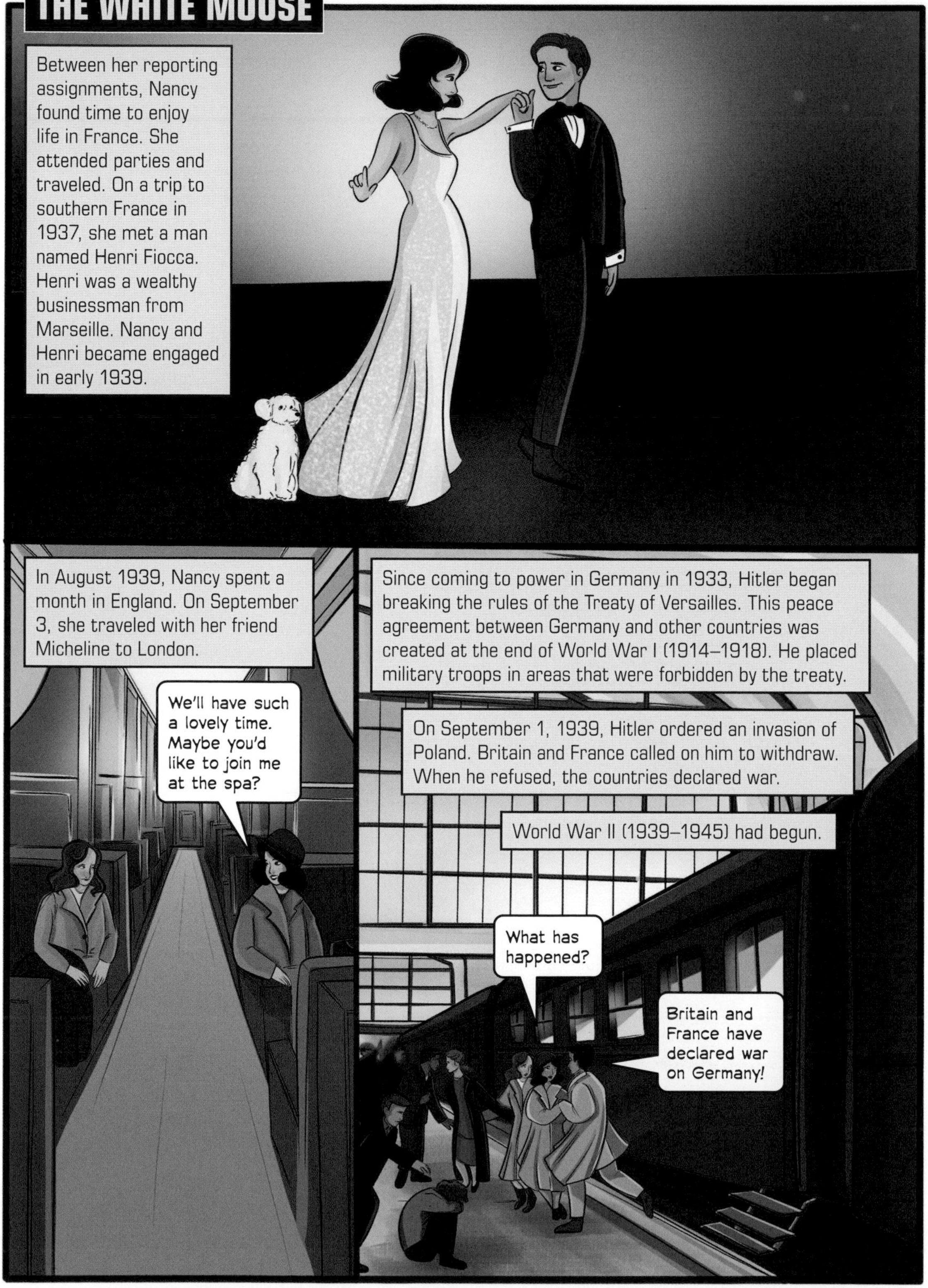
Between her reporting assignments, Nancy found time to enjoy life in France. She attended parties and traveled. On a trip to southern France in 1937, she met a man named Henri Fiocca. Henri was a wealthy businessman from Marseille. Nancy and Henri became engaged in early 1939.
In August 1939, Nancy spent a month in England. On September 3, she traveled with her friend Micheline to London.
We'll have such a lovely time. Maybe you'd like to join me at the spa?
Since coming to power in Germany in 1933, Hitler began breaking the rules of the Treaty of Versailles. This peace agreement between Germany and other countries was created at the end of World War I (1914–1918). He placed military troops in areas that were forbidden by the treaty.
On September 1, 1939, Hitler ordered an invasion of Poland. Britain and France called on him to withdraw. When he refused, the countries declared war.
World War II (1939–1945) had begun.
What has happened?
Britain and France have declared war on Germany!

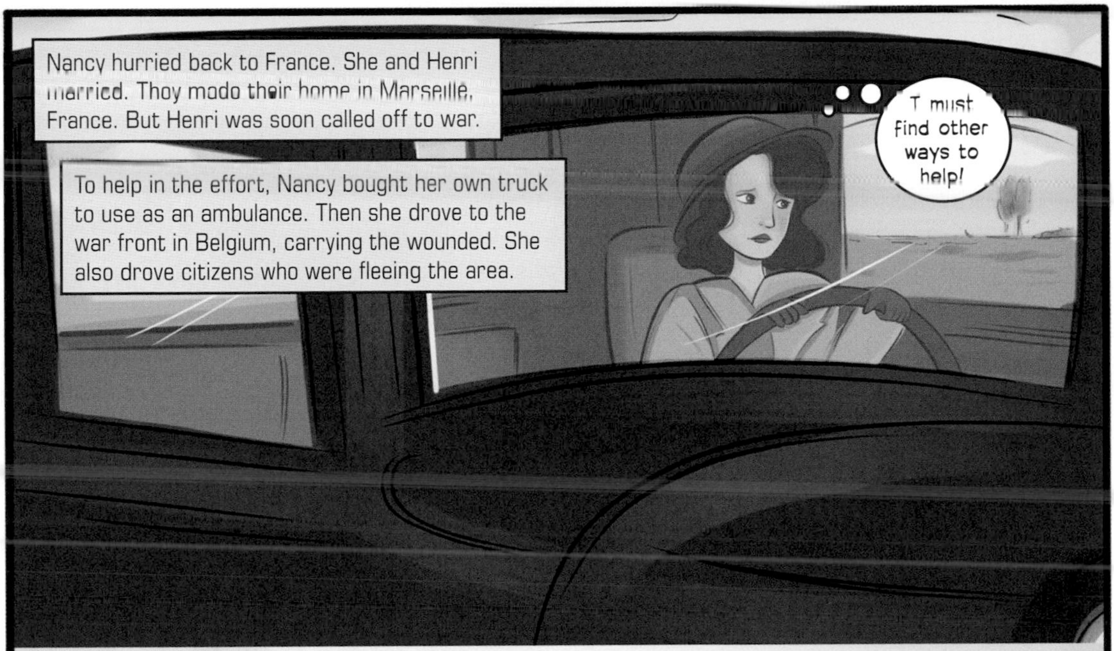
Nancy hurried back to France. She and Henri married. They made their home in Marseille, France. But Henri was soon called off to war.
To help in the effort, Nancy bought her own truck to use as an ambulance. Then she drove to the war front in Belgium, carrying the wounded. She also drove citizens who were fleeing the area.
I must find other ways to help!

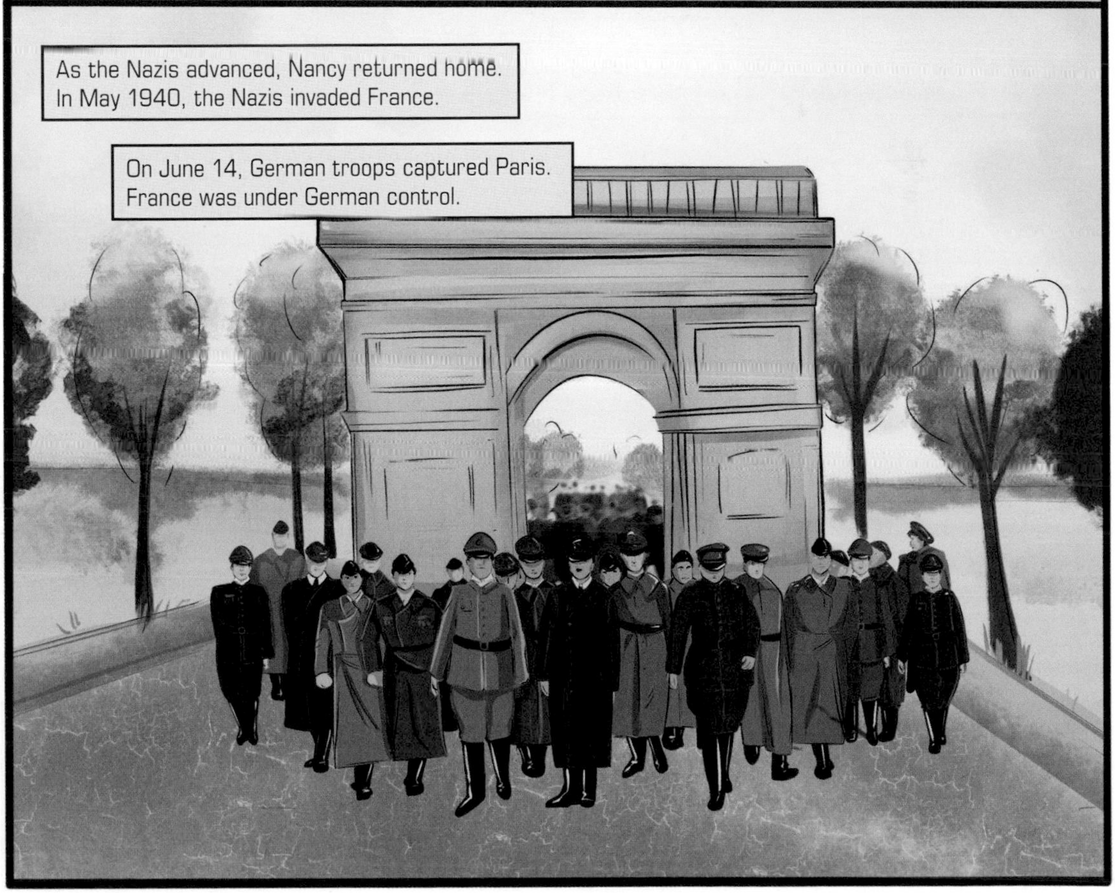
As the Nazis advanced, Nancy returned home. In May 1940, the Nazis invaded France.
On June 14, German troops captured Paris. France was under German control.

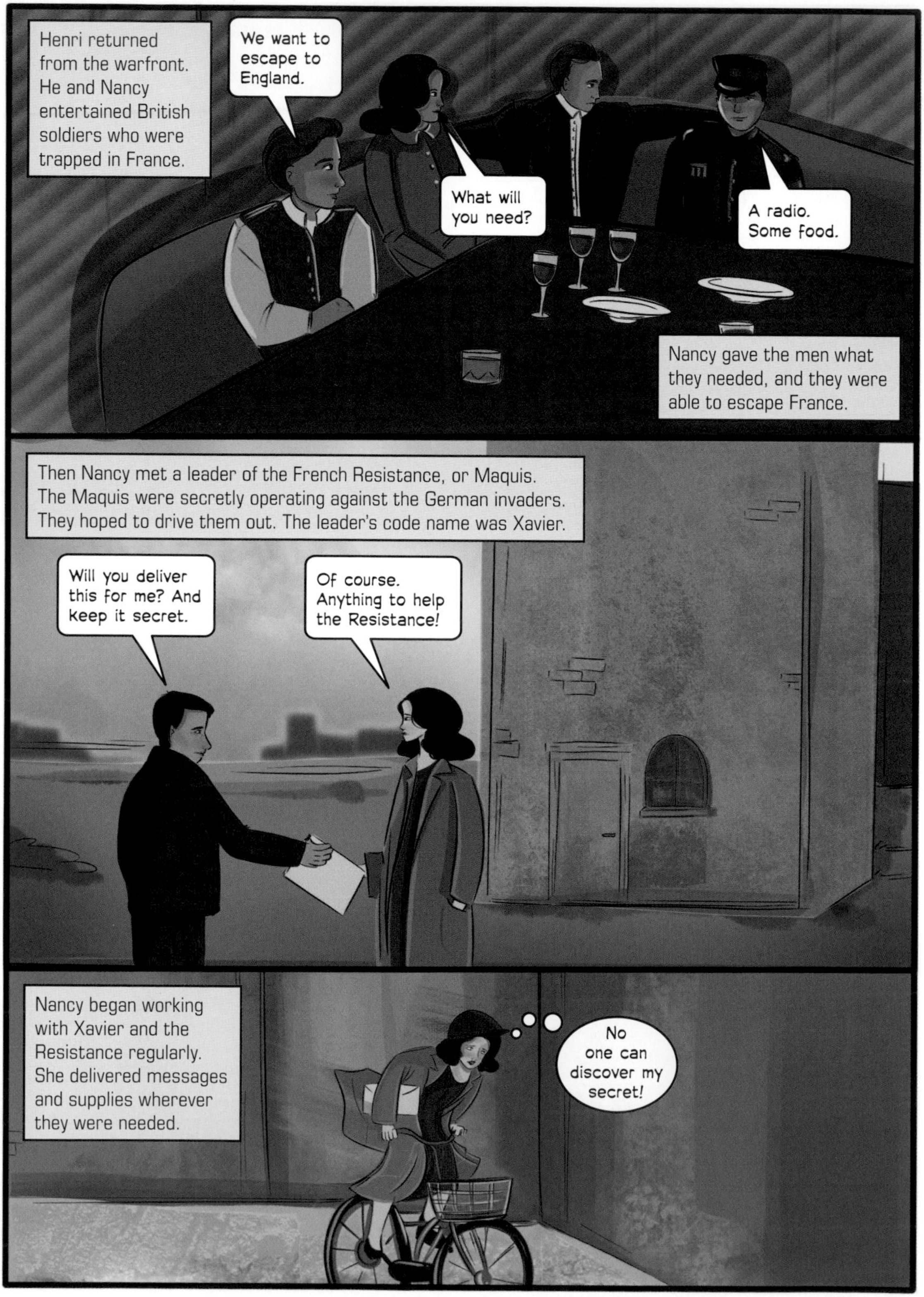

Henri returned from the warfront. He and Nancy entertained British soldiers who were trapped in France.
We want to escape to England.
What will you need?
A radio. Some food.
Nancy gave the men what they needed, and they were able to escape France.
Then Nancy met a leader of the French Resistance, or Maquis. The Maquis were secretly operating against the German invaders. They hoped to drive them out. The leader's code name was Xavier.
Will you deliver this for me? And keep it secret.
Of course. Anything to help the Resistance!
Nancy began working with Xavier and the Resistance regularly. She delivered messages and supplies wherever they were needed.
No one can discover my secret!

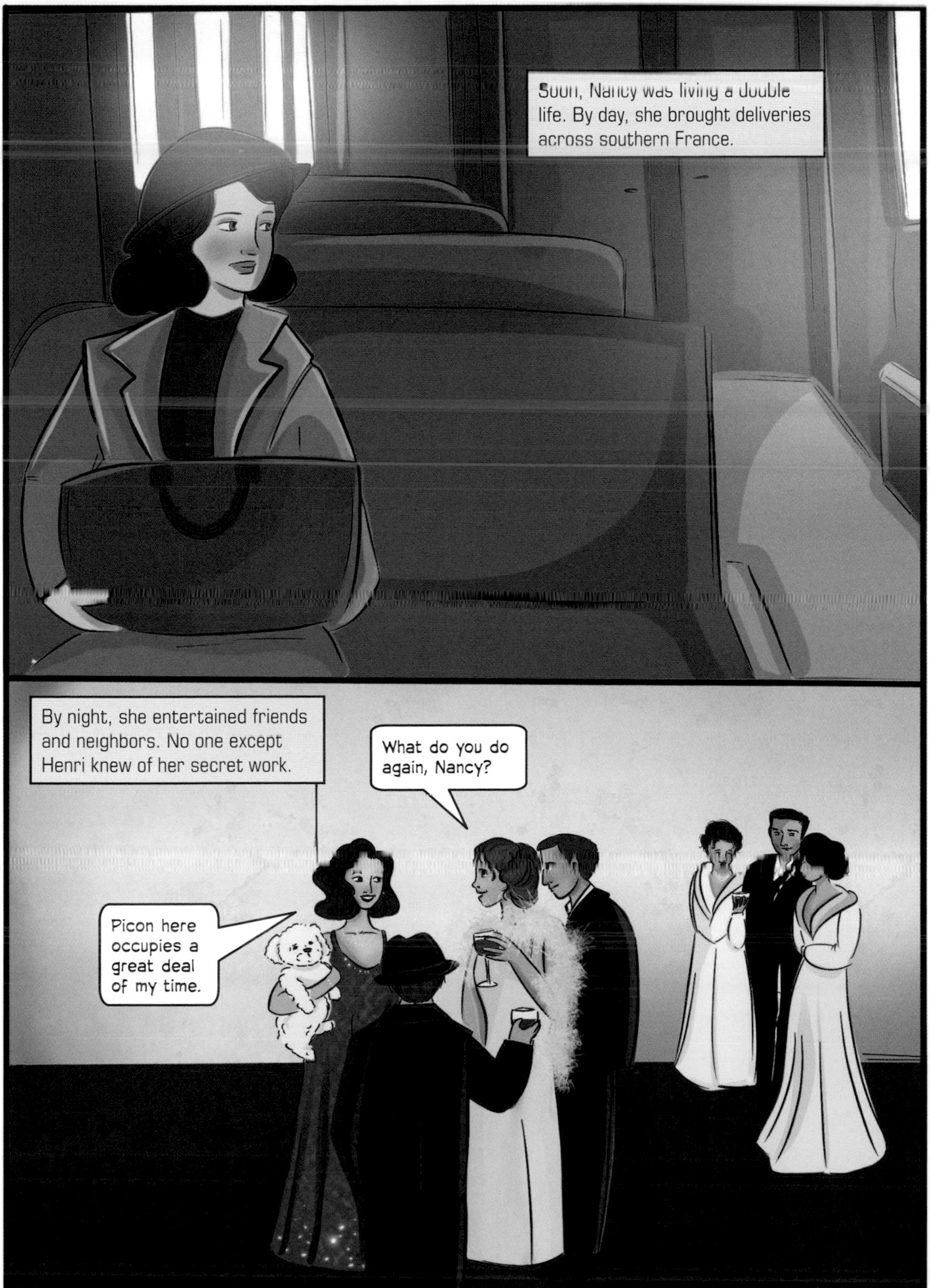
Soon, Nancy was living a double life. By day, she brought deliveries across southern France.
By night, she entertained friends and neighbors. No one except Henri knew of her secret work.
What do you do again, Nancy?
Picon here occupies a great deal of my time.

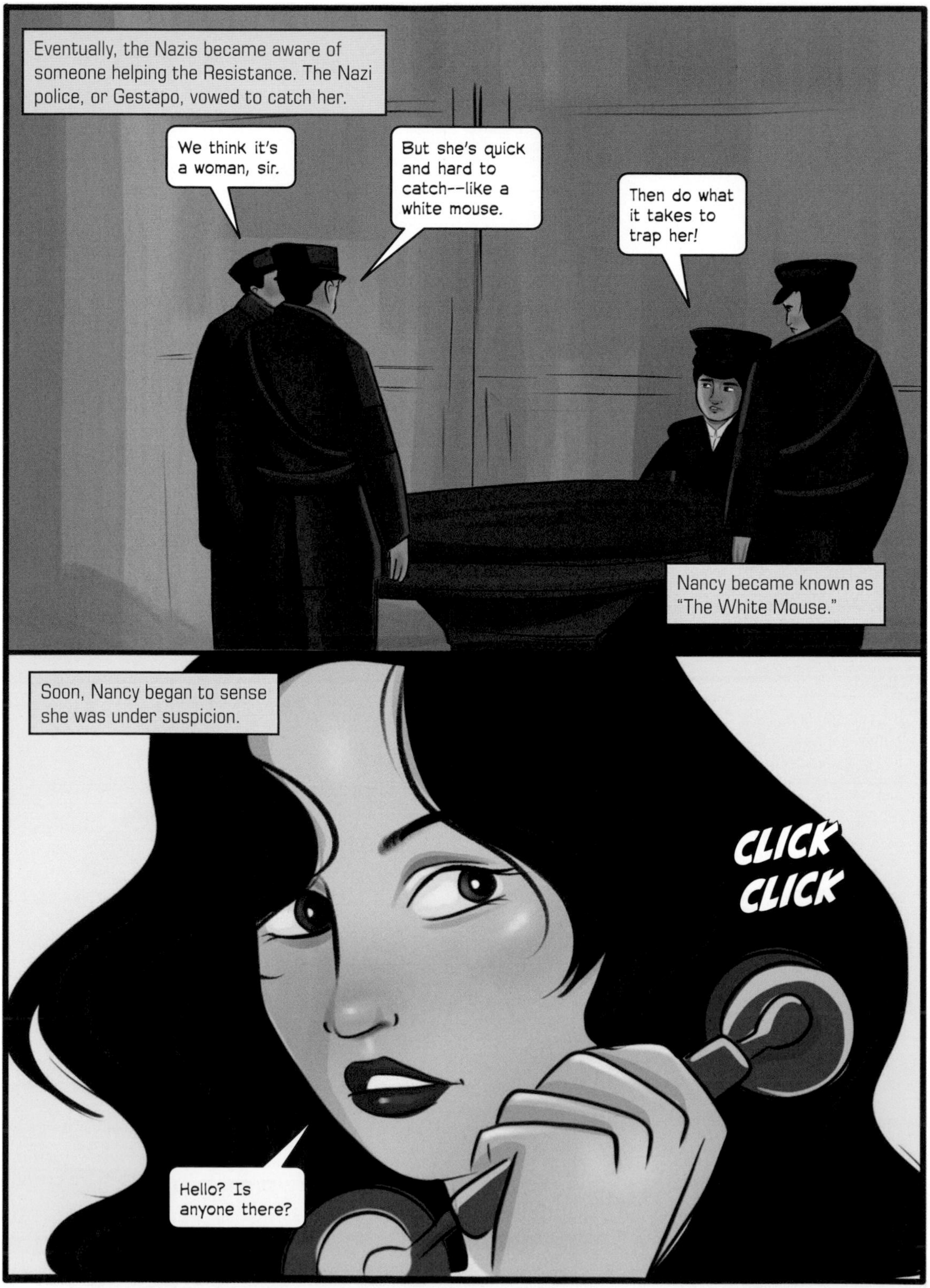
Eventually, the Nazis became aware of someone helping the Resistance. The Nazi police, or Gestapo, vowed to catch her.
We think it's a woman, sir.
But she's quick and hard to catch--like a white mouse.
Then do what it takes to trap her!
Nancy became known as "The White Mouse."
Soon, Nancy began to sense she was under suspicion.
CLICK CLICK
Hello? Is anyone there?

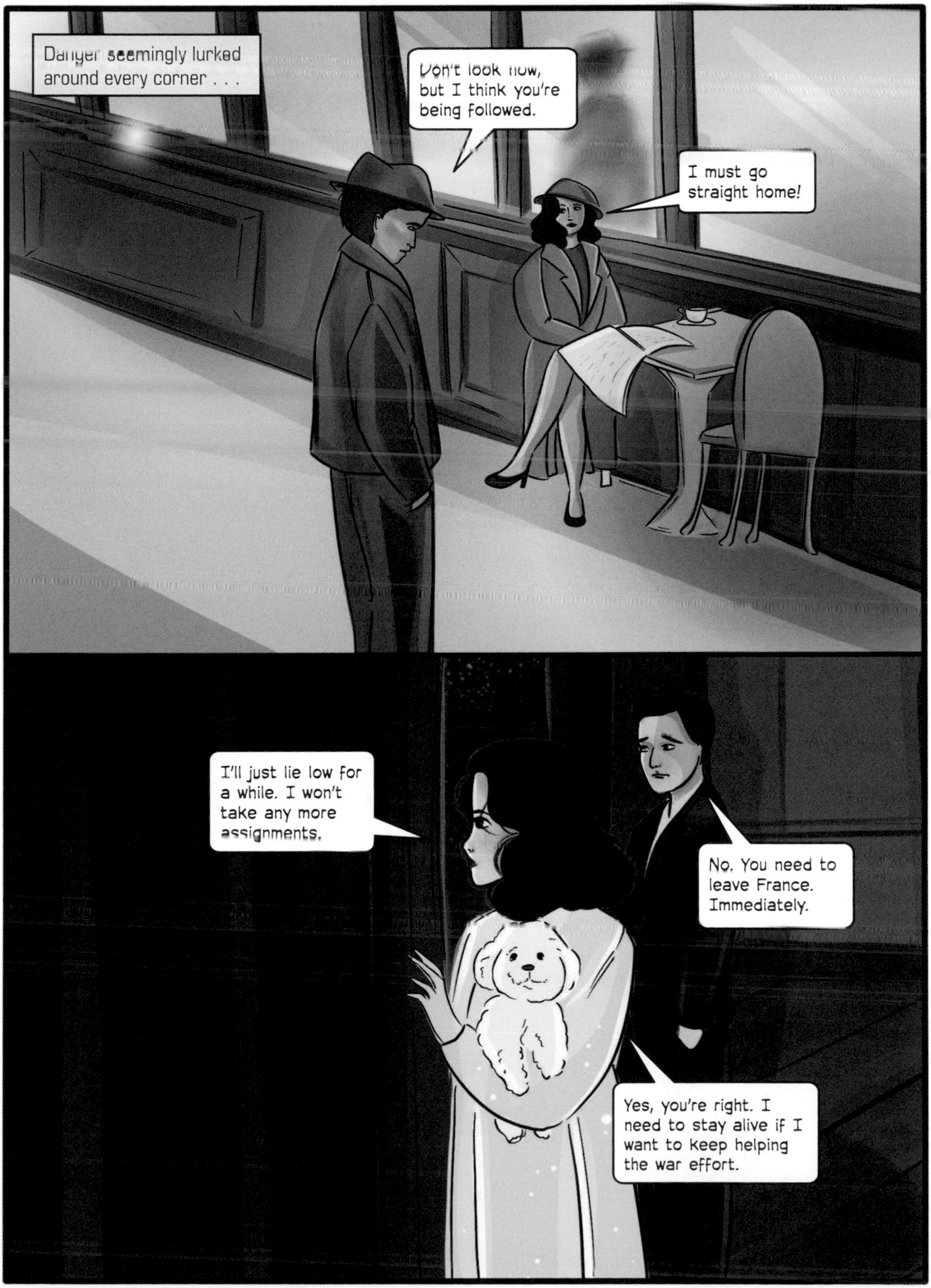
Danger seemingly lurked around every corner . . .
Don't look now, but I think you're being followed.
I must go straight home!
I'll just lie low for a while. I won't take any more assignments.
No. You need to leave France. Immediately.
Yes, you're right. I need to stay alive if I want to keep helping the war effort.

ESCAPE AND RETURN

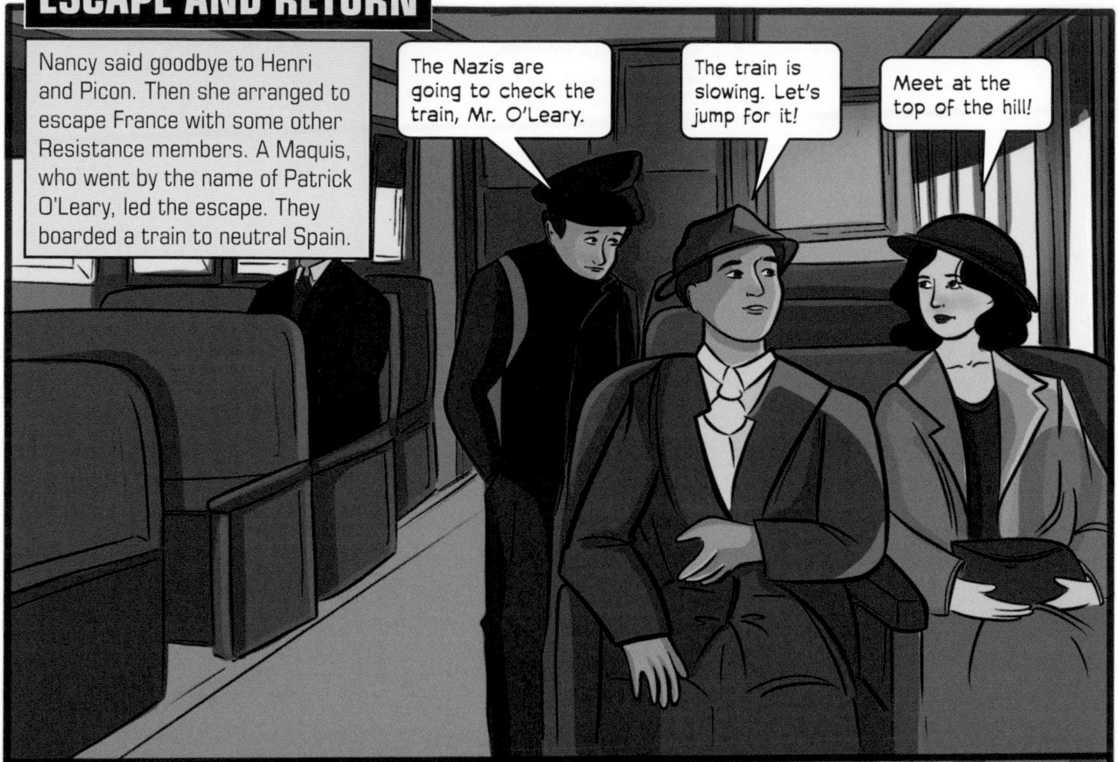
Nancy said goodbye to Henri and Picon. Then she arranged to escape France with some other Resistance members. A Maquis, who went by the name of Patrick O'Leary, led the escape. They boarded a train to neutral Spain.
The Nazis are going to check the train, Mr. O'Leary.
The train is slowing. Let's jump for it!
Meet at the top of the hill!

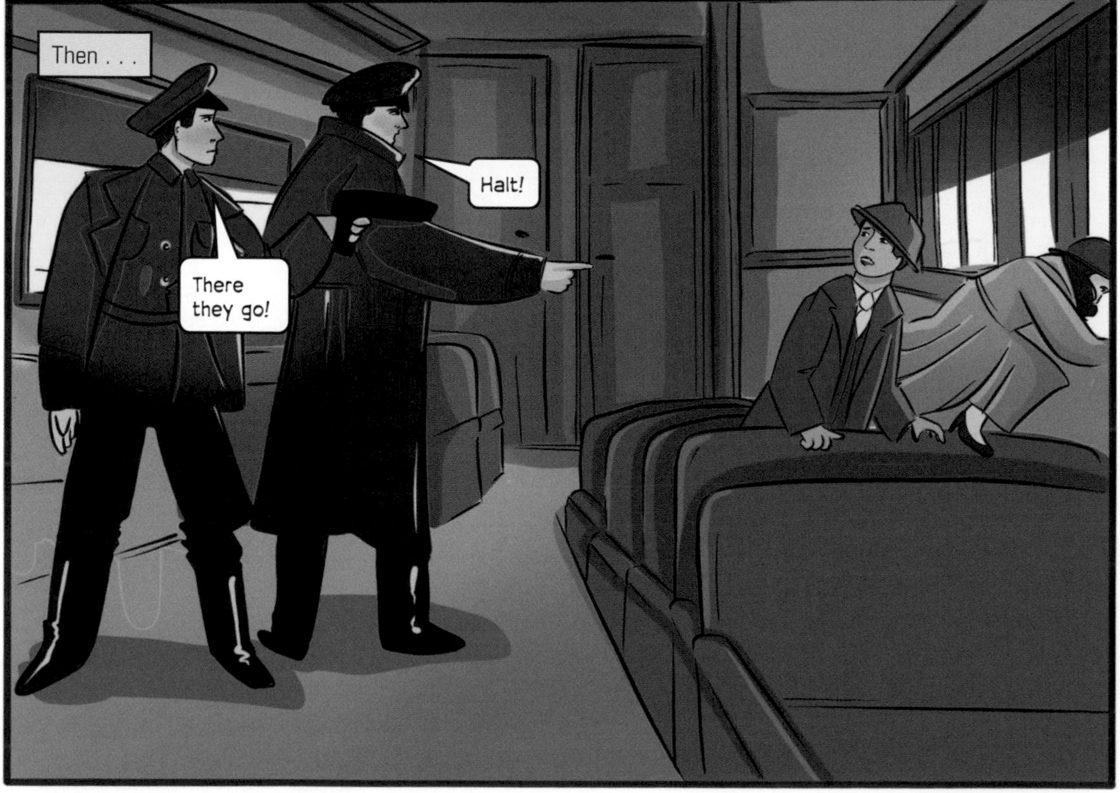
Then . . .
Halt!
There they go!

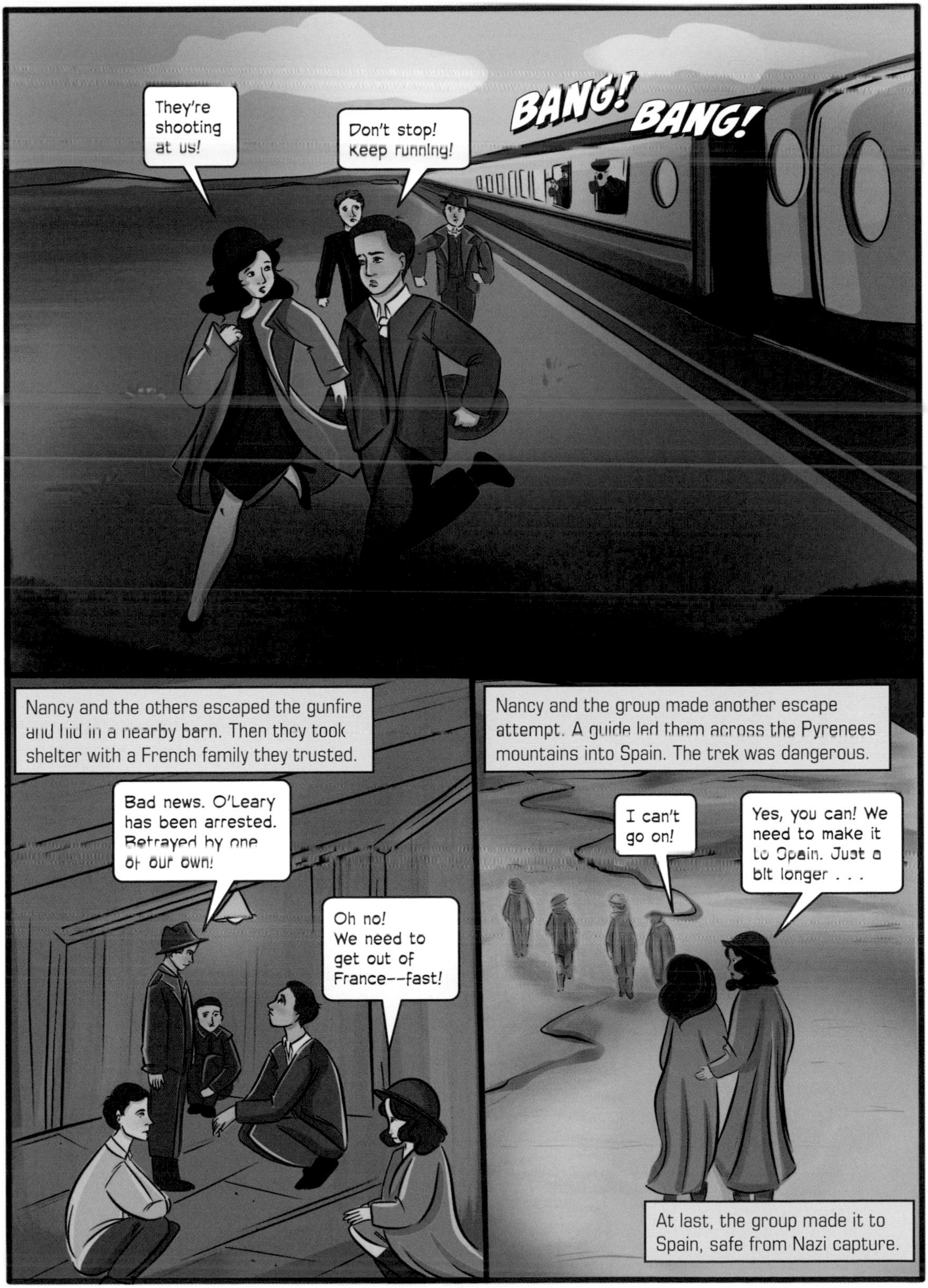
They're shooting at us!
Don't stop! Keep running!
BANG! BANG!
Nancy and the others escaped the gunfire and hid in a nearby barn. Then they took shelter with a French family they trusted.
Bad news. O'Leary has been arrested. Betrayed by one of our own!
Oh no! We need to get out of France--fast!
Nancy and the group made another escape attempt. A guide led them across the Pyrenees mountains into Spain. The trek was dangerous.
I can't go on!
Yes, you can! We need to make it to Spain. Just a bit longer . . .
At last, the group made it to Spain, safe from Nazi capture.

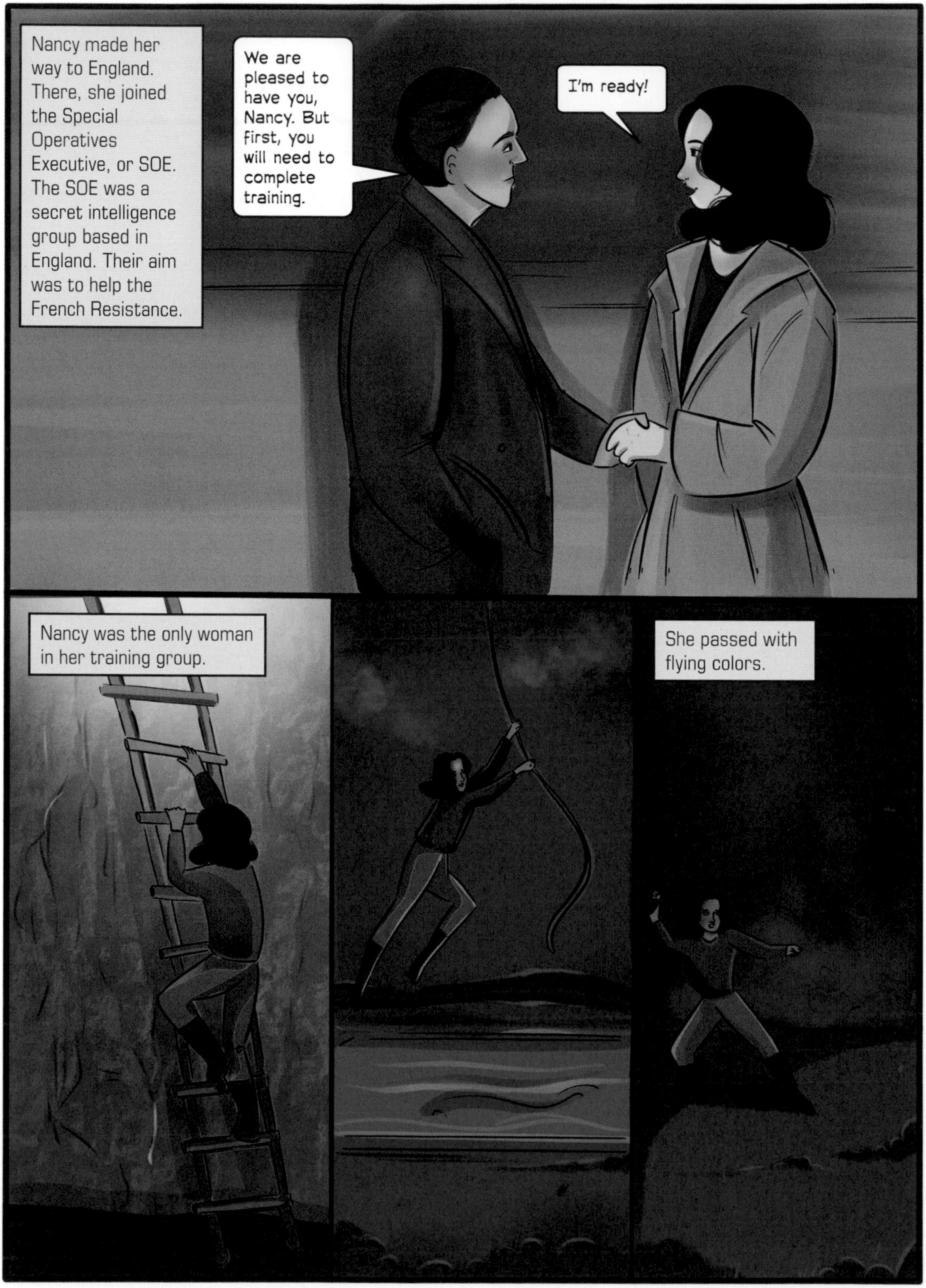
Nancy made her way to England. There, she joined the Special Operatives Executive, or SOE. The SOE was a secret intelligence group based in England. Their aim was to help the French Resistance.
We are pleased to have you, Nancy. But first, you will need to complete training.
I'm ready!
Nancy was the only woman in her training group.
She passed with flying colors.

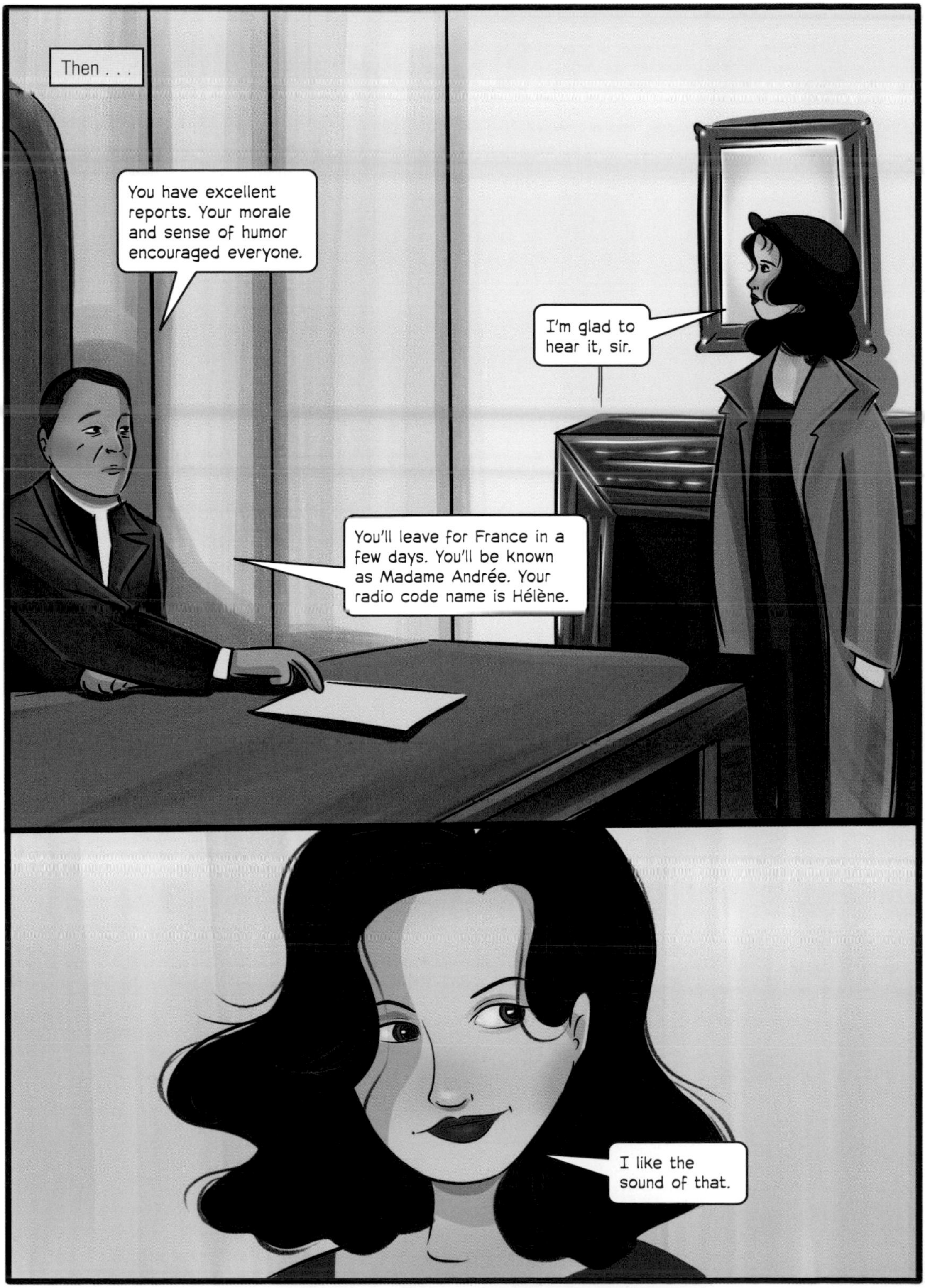
Then . . .
You have excellent reports. Your morale and sense of humor encouraged everyone.
I'm glad to hear it, sir.
You'll leave for France in a few days. You'll be known as Madame Andrée. Your radio code name is Hélène.
I like the sound of that.

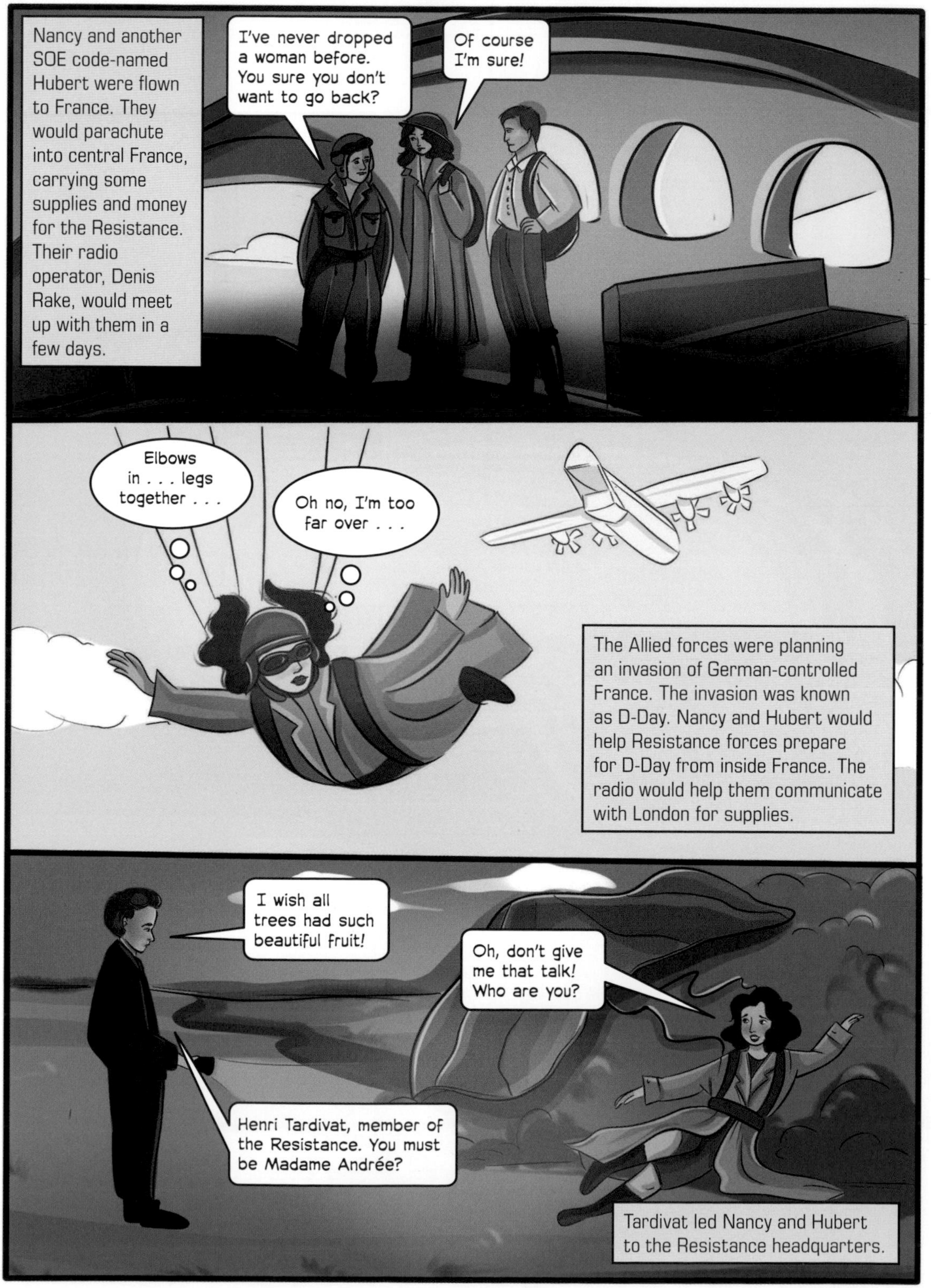
Nancy and another SOE code-named Hubert were flown to France. They would parachute into central France, carrying some supplies and money for the Resistance. Their radio operator, Denis Rake, would meet up with them in a few days.
I've never dropped a woman before. You sure you don't want to go back?
Of course I'm sure!
Elbows in . . . legs together . . .
Oh no, I'm too far over . . .
The Allied forces were planning an invasion of German-controlled France. The invasion was known as D-Day. Nancy and Hubert would help Resistance forces prepare for D-Day from inside France. The radio would help them communicate with London for supplies.
I wish all trees had such beautiful fruit!
Oh, don't give me that talk! Who are you?
Henri Tardivat, member of the Resistance. You must be Madame Andrée?
Tardivat led Nancy and Hubert to the Resistance headquarters.

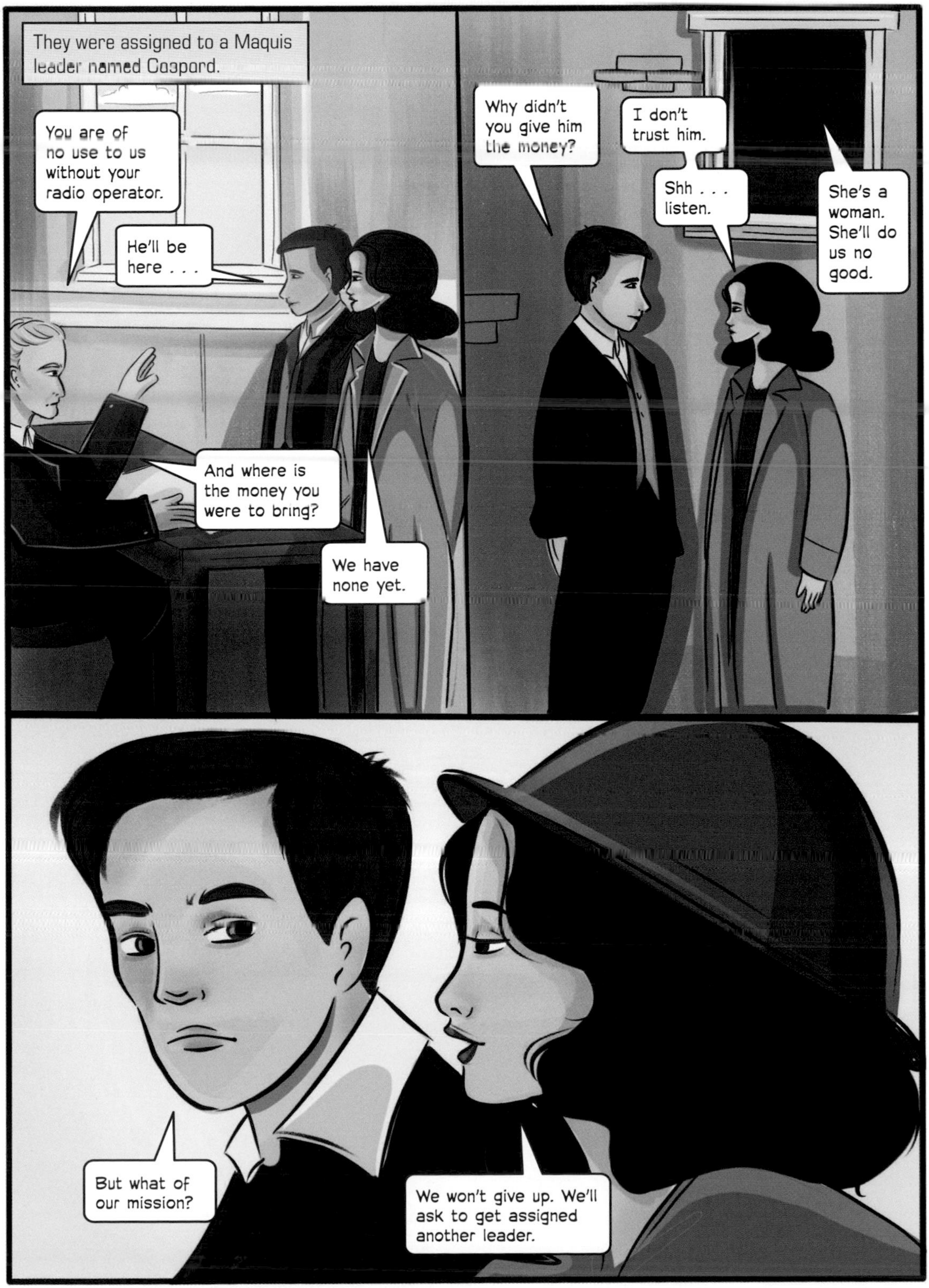
They were assigned to a Maquis leader named Caspard.
You are of no use to us without your radio operator.
He'll be here . . .
And where is the money you were to bring?
We have none yet.
Why didn't you give him the money?
I don't trust him.
Shh . . . listen.
She's a woman. She'll do us no good.
But what of our mission?
We won't give up. We'll ask to get assigned another leader.

CODE NAME "HÉLÈNE"

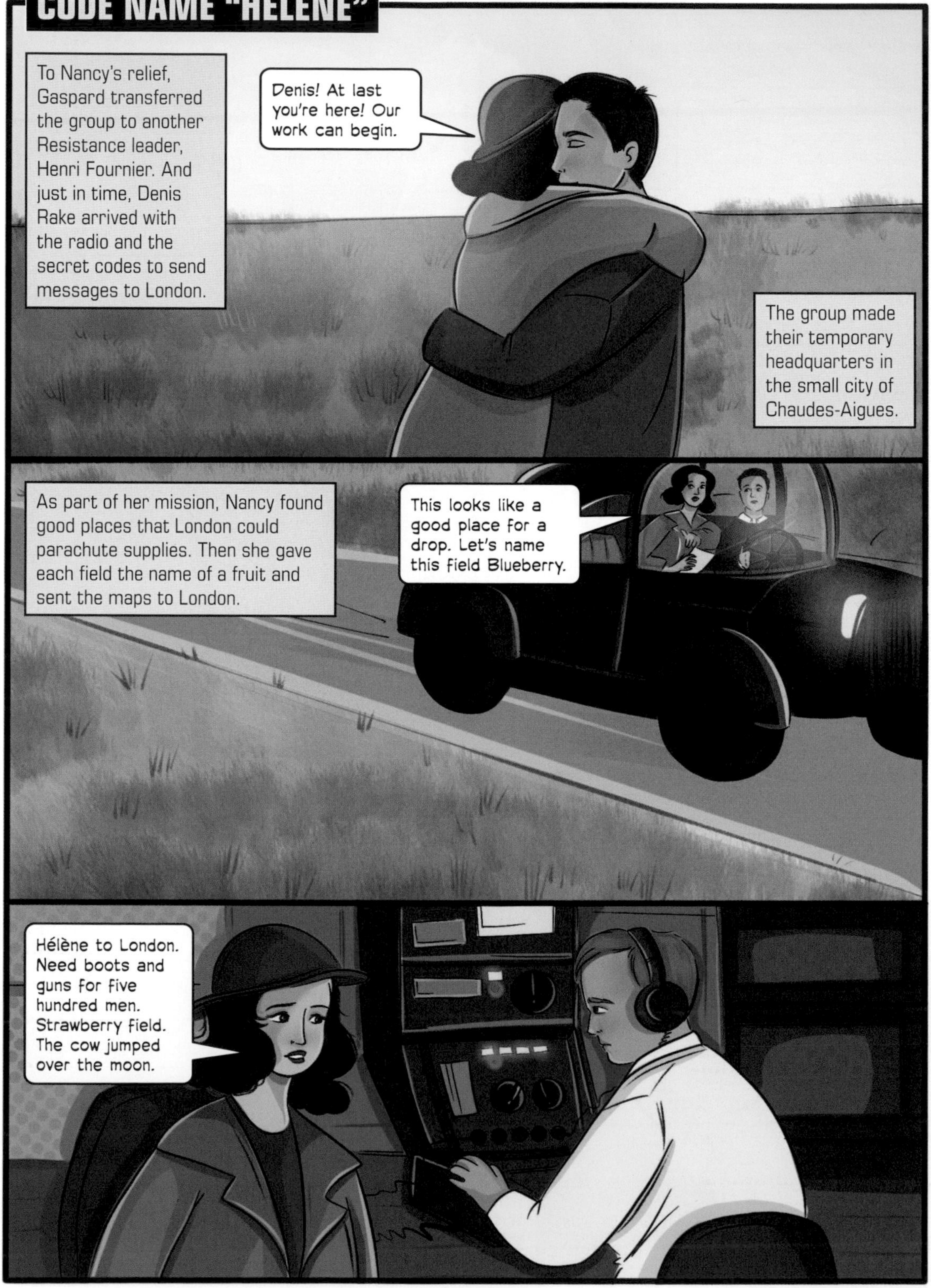
To Nancy's relief, Gaspard transferred the group to another Resistance leader, Henri Fournier. And just in time, Denis Rake arrived with the radio and the secret codes to send messages to London.
Denis! At last you're here! Our work can begin.
The group made their temporary headquarters in the small city of Chaudes-Aigues.
As part of her mission, Nancy found good places that London could parachute supplies. Then she gave each field the name of a fruit and sent the maps to London.
This looks like a good place for a drop. Let's name this field Blueberry.
Hélène to London. Need boots and guns for five hundred men. Strawberry field. The cow jumped over the moon.

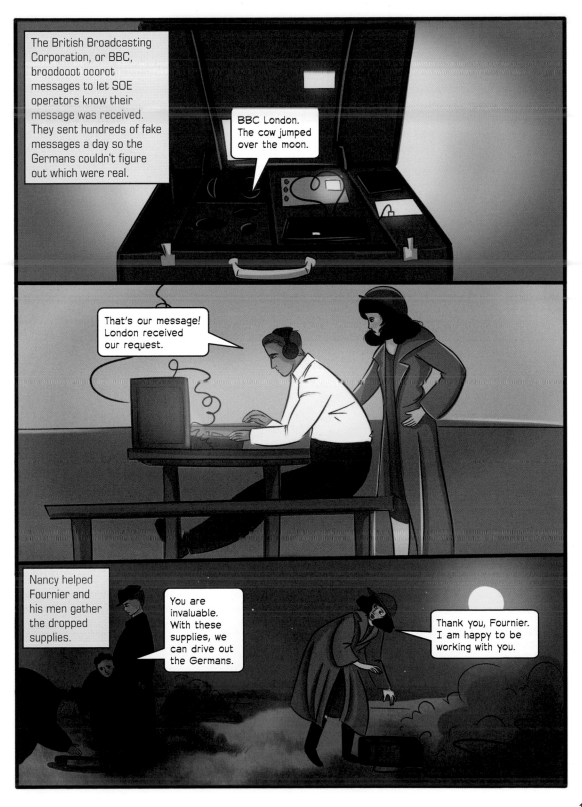

The British Broadcasting Corporation, or BBC, broadcast short messages to let SOE operators know their message was received. They sent hundreds of fake messages a day so the Germans couldn't figure out which were real.

BBC London. The cow jumped over the moon.

That's our message! London received our request.

Nancy helped Fournier and his men gather the dropped supplies.

You are invaluable. With these supplies, we can drive out the Germans.

Thank you, Fournier. I am happy to be working with you.

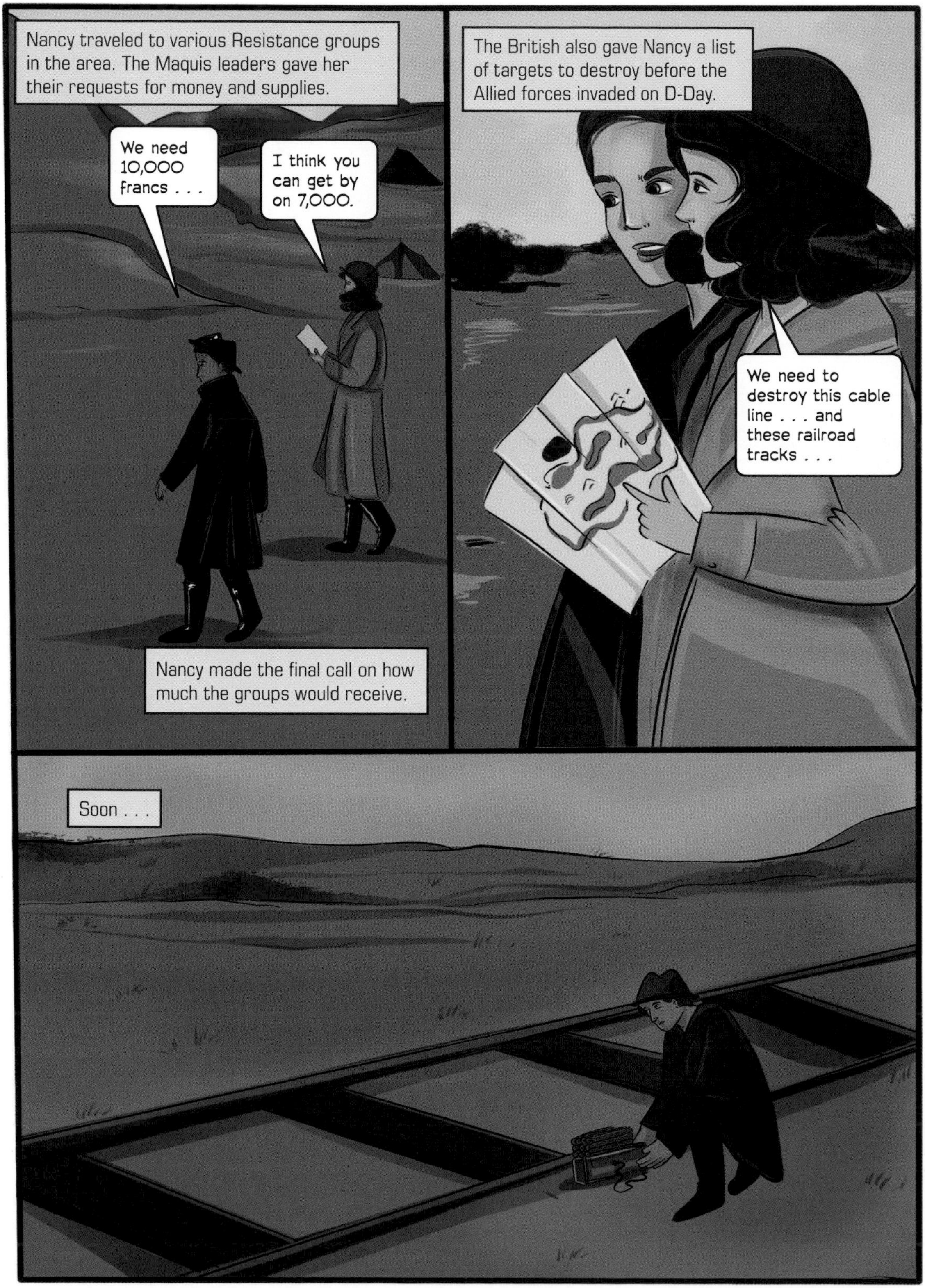
Nancy traveled to various Resistance groups in the area. The Maquis leaders gave her their requests for money and supplies.
We need 10,000 francs . . .
I think you can get by on 7,000.
Nancy made the final call on how much the groups would receive.
The British also gave Nancy a list of targets to destroy before the Allied forces invaded on D-Day.
We need to destroy this cable line . . . and these railroad tracks . . .
Soon . . .

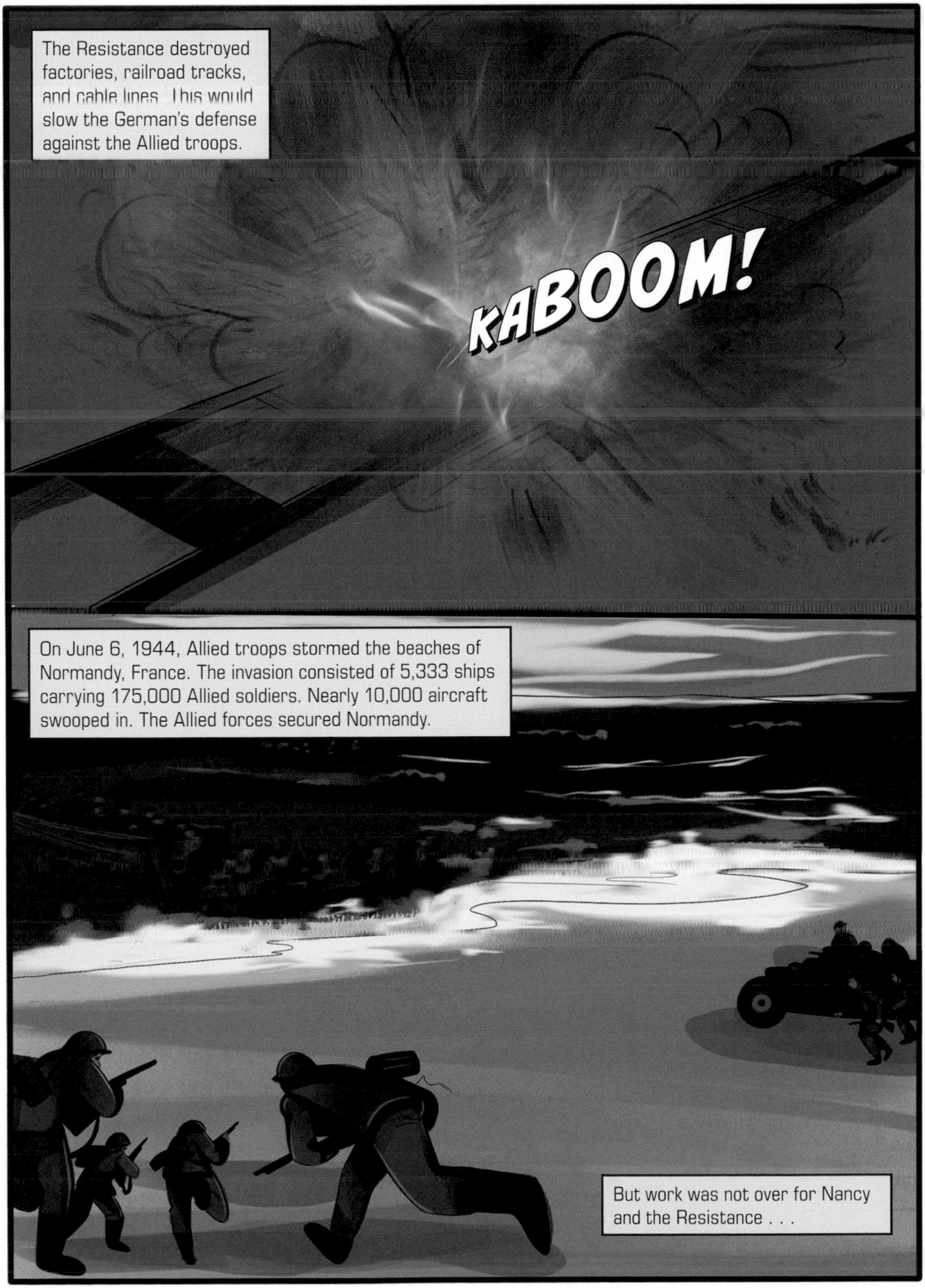
The Resistance destroyed factories, railroad tracks, and cable lines. This would slow the German's defense against the Allied troops.
KABOOM!
On June 6, 1944, Allied troops stormed the beaches of Normandy, France. The invasion consisted of 5,333 ships carrying 175,000 Allied soldiers. Nearly 10,000 aircraft swooped in. The Allied forces secured Normandy.
But work was not over for Nancy and the Resistance . . .

THE BICYCLE RIDE

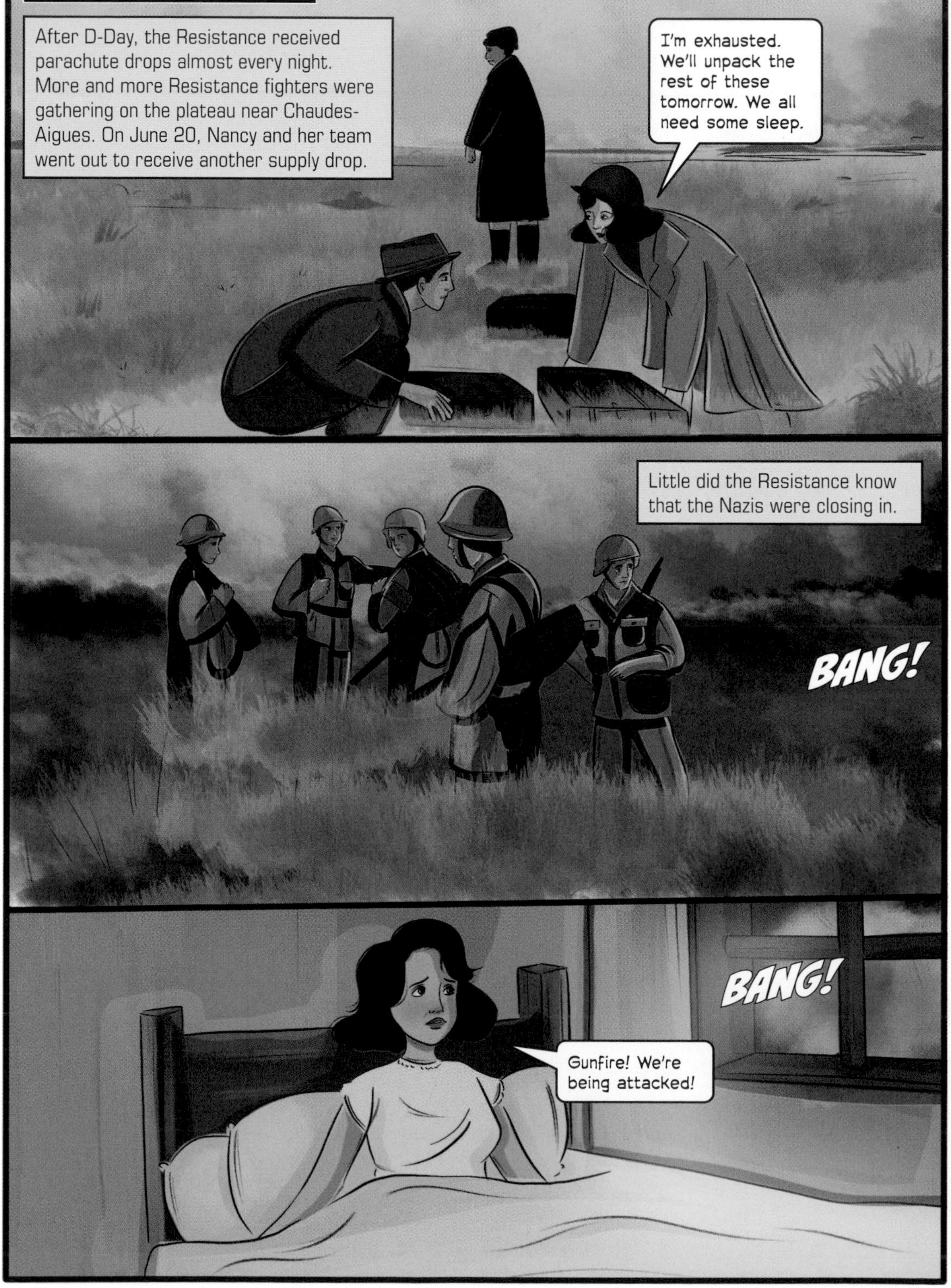
After D-Day, the Resistance received parachute drops almost every night. More and more Resistance fighters were gathering on the plateau near Chaudes-Aigues. On June 20, Nancy and her team went out to receive another supply drop.
I'm exhausted. We'll unpack the rest of these tomorrow. We all need some sleep.
Little did the Resistance know that the Nazis were closing in.
BANG!
BANG!
Gunfire! We're being attacked!

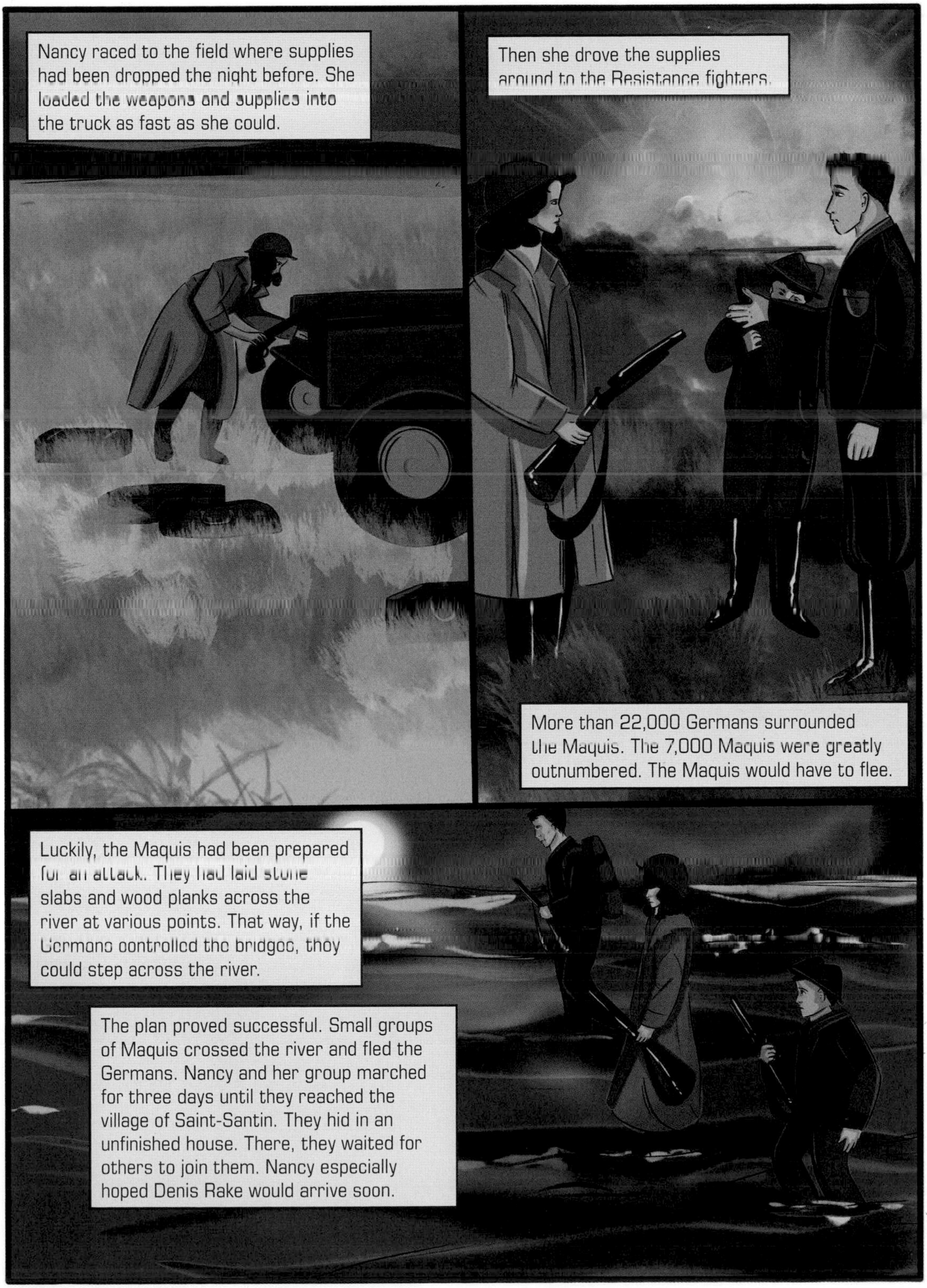
Nancy raced to the field where supplies had been dropped the night before. She loaded the weapons and supplies into the truck as fast as she could.
Then she drove the supplies around to the Resistance fighters.
More than 22,000 Germans surrounded the Maquis. The 7,000 Maquis were greatly outnumbered. The Maquis would have to flee.
Luckily, the Maquis had been prepared for an attack. They had laid stone slabs and wood planks across the river at various points. That way, if the Germans controlled the bridges, they could step across the river.
The plan proved successful. Small groups of Maquis crossed the river and fled the Germans. Nancy and her group marched for three days until they reached the village of Saint-Santin. They hid in an unfinished house. There, they waited for others to join them. Nancy especially hoped Denis Rake would arrive soon.

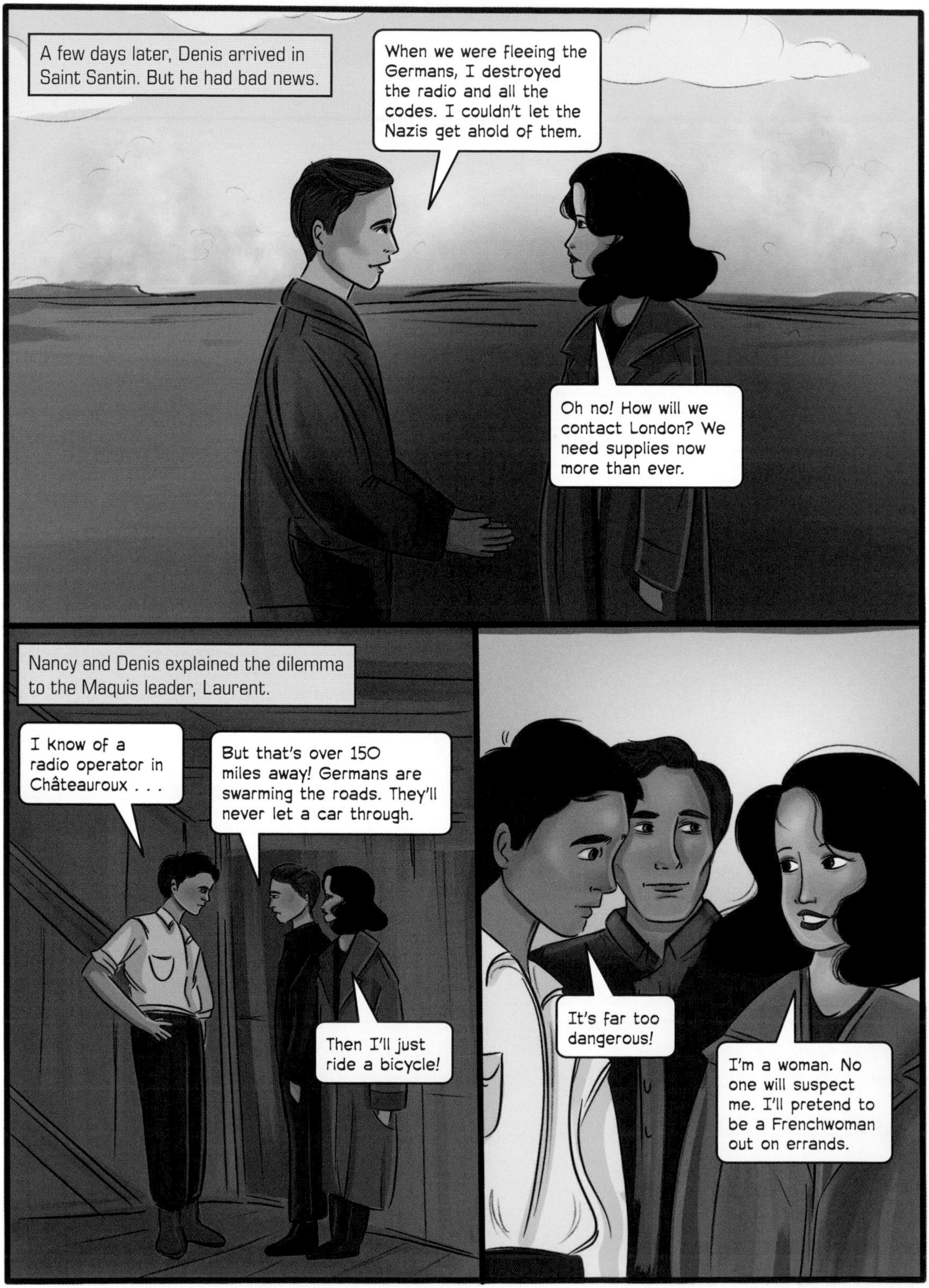

A few days later, Denis arrived in Saint Santin. But he had bad news.
When we were fleeing the Germans, I destroyed the radio and all the codes. I couldn't let the Nazis get ahold of them.
Oh no! How will we contact London? We need supplies now more than ever.
Nancy and Denis explained the dilemma to the Maquis leader, Laurent.
I know of a radio operator in Châteauroux . . .
But that's over 150 miles away! Germans are swarming the roads. They'll never let a car through.
Then I'll just ride a bicycle!
It's far too dangerous!
I'm a woman. No one will suspect me. I'll pretend to be a Frenchwoman out on errands.

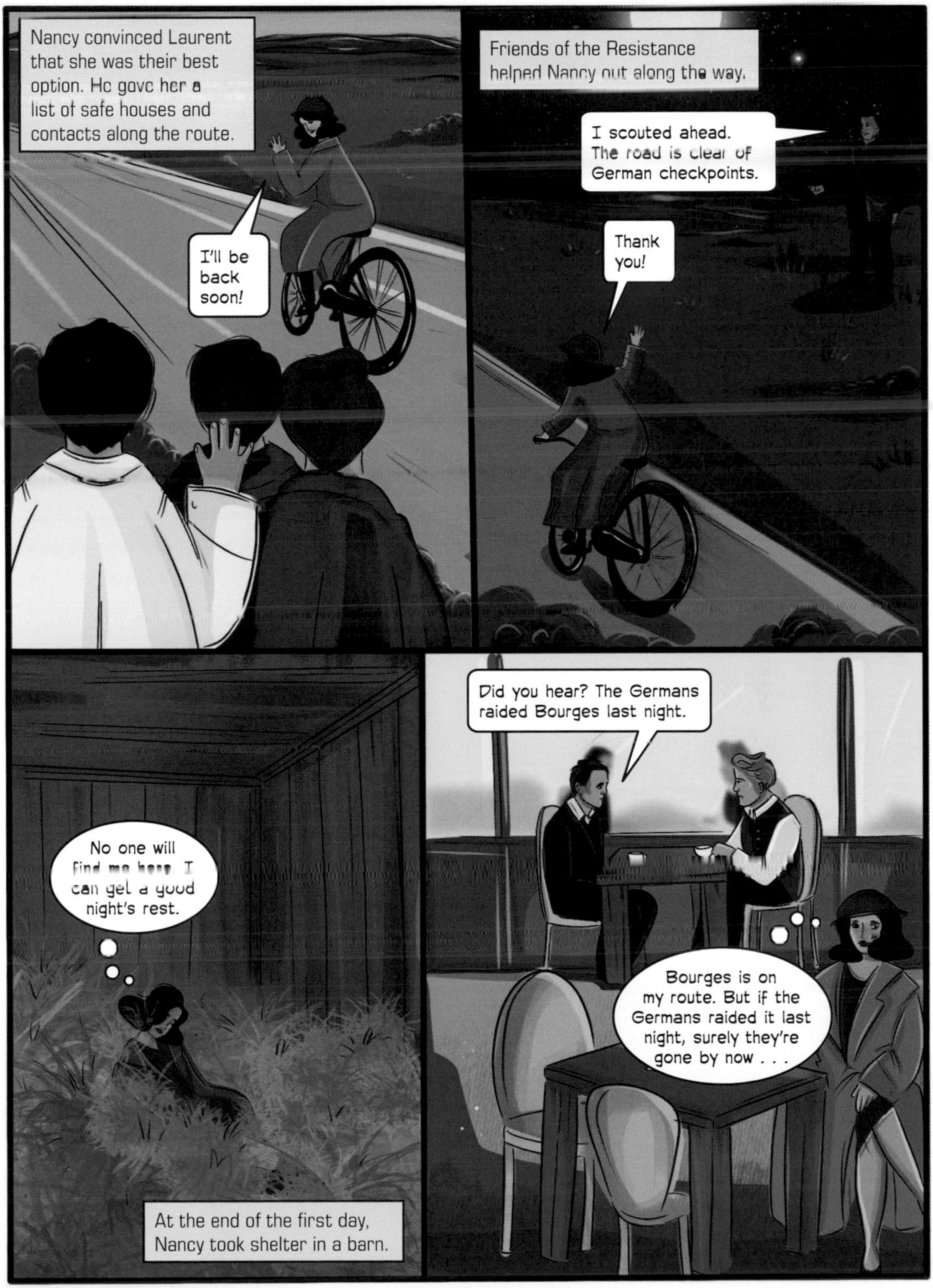

Nancy convinced Laurent that she was their best option. He gave her a list of safe houses and contacts along the route.
I'll be back soon!
Friends of the Resistance helped Nancy out along the way.
I scouted ahead. The road is clear of German checkpoints.
Thank you!
No one will find me here. I can get a good night's rest.
At the end of the first day, Nancy took shelter in a barn.
Did you hear? The Germans raided Bourges last night.
Bourges is on my route. But if the Germans raided it last night, surely they're gone by now . . .

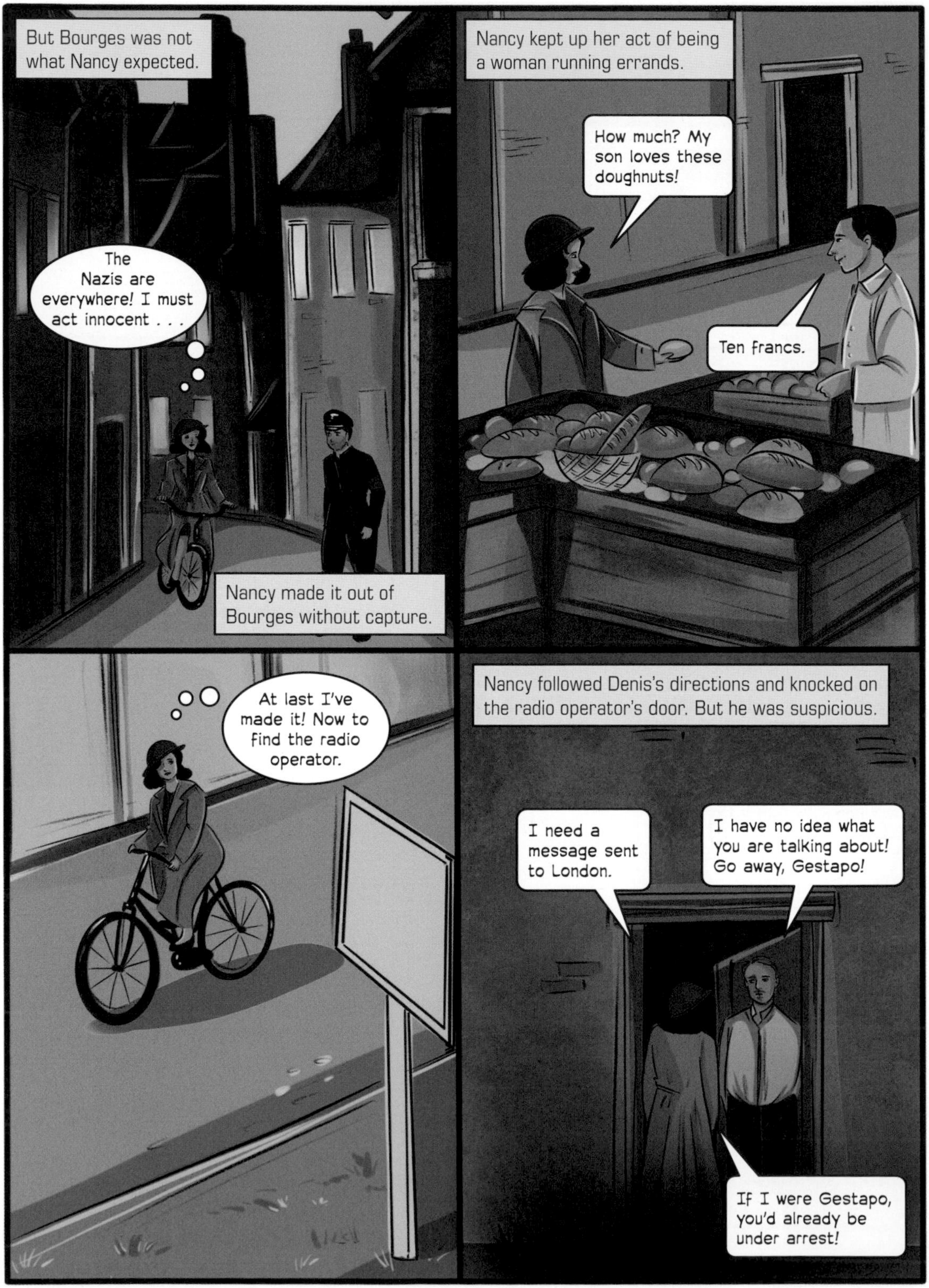

But Bourges was not what Nancy expected.
The Nazis are everywhere! I must act innocent . . .
Nancy made it out of Bourges without capture.
Nancy kept up her act of being a woman running errands.
How much? My son loves these doughnuts!
Ten francs.
At last I've made it! Now to find the radio operator.
Nancy followed Denis's directions and knocked on the radio operator's door. But he was suspicious.
I need a message sent to London.
I have no idea what you are talking about! Go away, Gestapo!
If I were Gestapo, you'd already be under arrest!

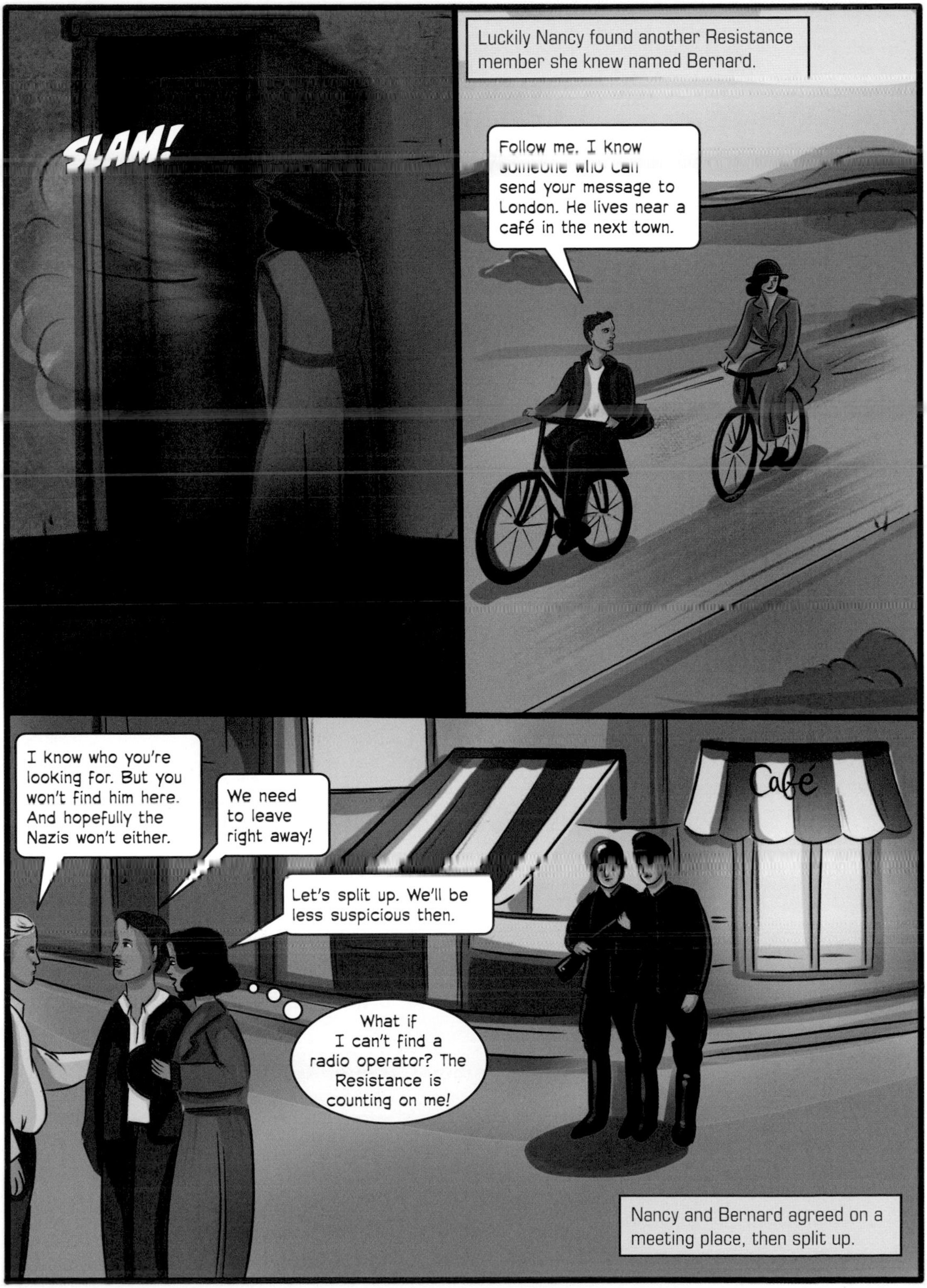
SLAM!
Luckily Nancy found another Resistance member she knew named Bernard.
Follow me. I know someone who can send your message to London. He lives near a café in the next town.
I know who you're looking for. But you won't find him here. And hopefully the Nazis won't either.
We need to leave right away!
Let's split up. We'll be less suspicious then.
What if I can't find a radio operator? The Resistance is counting on me!
Café
Nancy and Bernard agreed on a meeting place, then split up.

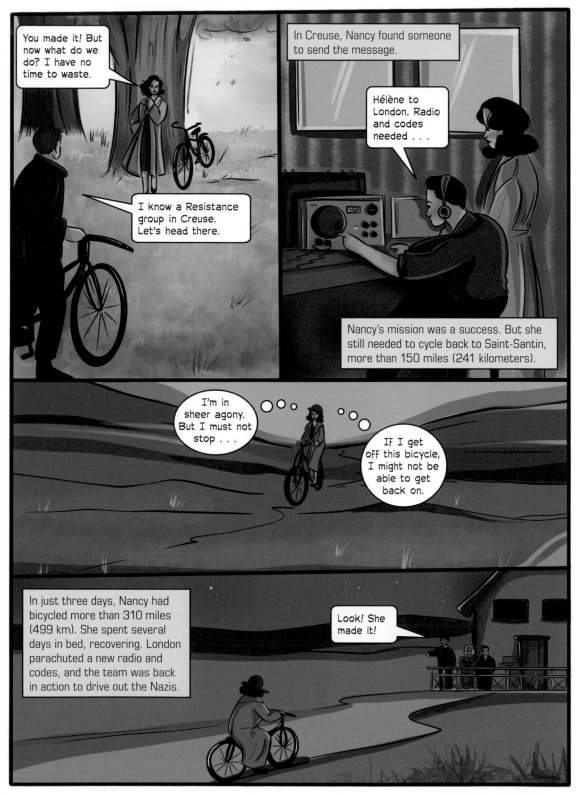

You made it! But now what do we do? I have no time to waste.

I know a Resistance group in Creuse. Let's head there.

In Creuse, Nancy found someone to send the message.

Hélène to London. Radio and codes needed . . .

Nancy's mission was a success. But she still needed to cycle back to Saint-Santin, more than 150 miles (241 kilometers).

I'm in sheer agony. But I must not stop . . .

If I get off this bicycle, I might not be able to get back on.

In just three days, Nancy had bicycled more than 310 miles (499 km). She spent several days in bed, recovering. London parachuted a new radio and codes, and the team was back in action to drive out the Nazis.

Look! She made it!

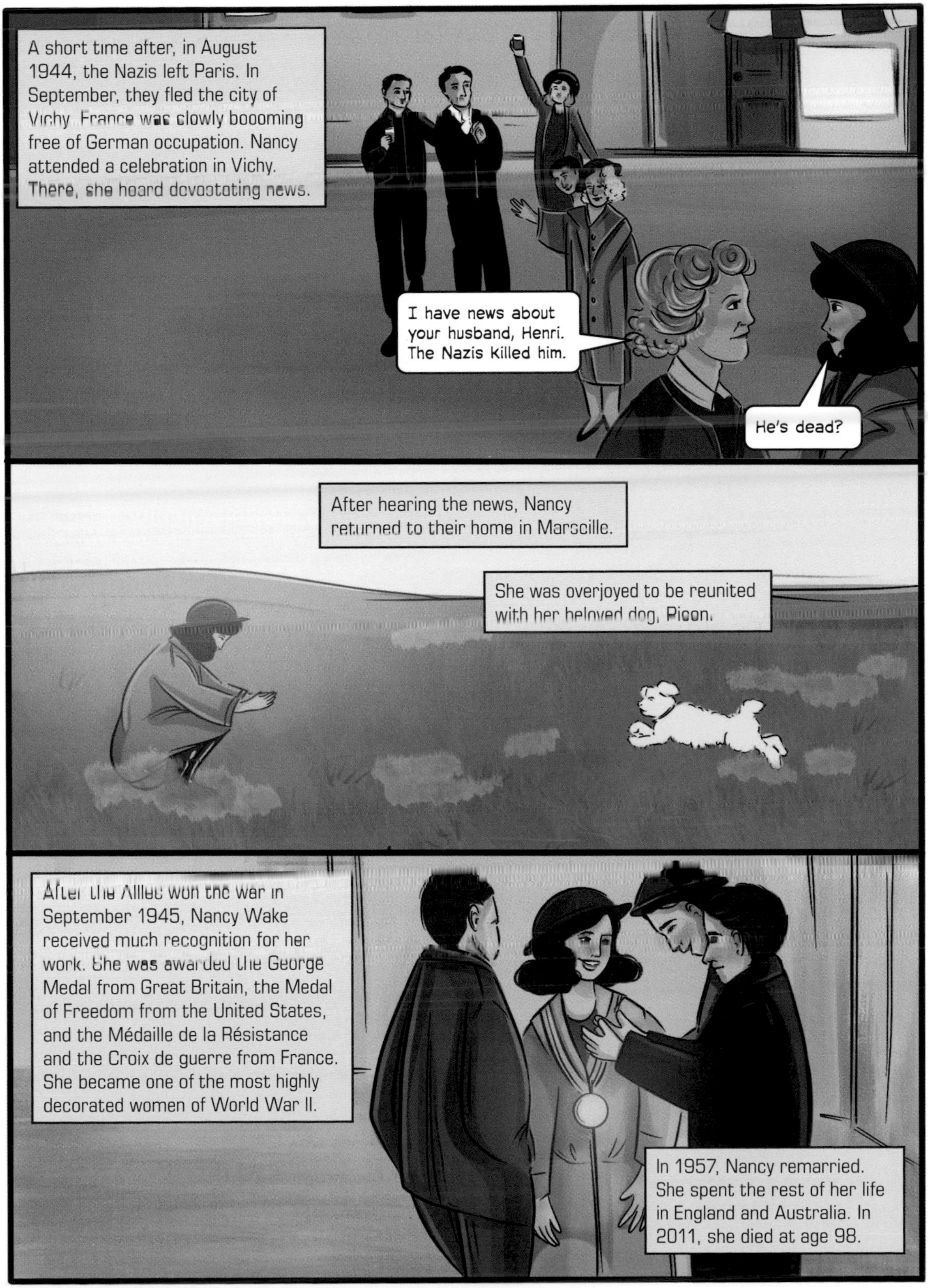
A short time after, in August 1944, the Nazis left Paris. In September, they fled the city of Vichy. France was slowly becoming free of German occupation. Nancy attended a celebration in Vichy. There, she heard devastating news.
I have news about your husband, Henri. The Nazis killed him.
He's dead?
After hearing the news, Nancy returned to their home in Marseille.
She was overjoyed to be reunited with her beloved dog, Picon.
After the Allies won the war in September 1945, Nancy Wake received much recognition for her work. She was awarded the George Medal from Great Britain, the Medal of Freedom from the United States, and the Médaille de la Résistance and the Croix de guerre from France. She became one of the most highly decorated women of World War II.
In 1957, Nancy remarried. She spent the rest of her life in England and Australia. In 2011, she died at age 98.

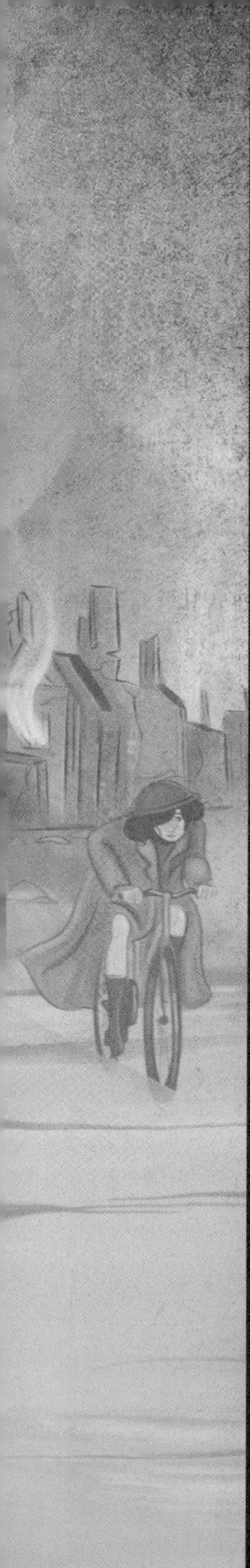

GLOSSARY

Allied (AL-ide)—a group of countries fighting together in World War II, including the United States, France, Great Britain, and the Soviet Union

checkpoint (CHEK POINT)—a point or stop where a security check is carried out

code name (COHD NAYM)—a name that has a secret meaning

Gestapo (geh-STAH-poh)—a secret-police organization employing underhanded and terrorist methods against persons suspected of disloyalty

invasion (in-VAY-zhun)—entrance of an army into a country for conquest

Maquis (mah-KEE)—a guerrilla fighter in the French underground during World War II

Nazi (NAHT-zee)—a member of the German fascist party controlling Germany from 1933 to 1945

neutral (NOO-truhl)—not favoring either side in a war

occupation (ok-yuh-PAY-shuhn)—the taking possession and control of an area

plateau (pla-TOH)—a broad, flat area of high land

safe house (SAYF-HOWSS)—a place where one may engage in secret activities or take refuge

suspicion (suh-SPISH-uhn)—the act or an instance of suspecting or being suspected

READ MORE

Milco, John C. *Fighting Forces of World War II on the Home Front.* North Mankato, MN: Capstone, 2020.

Roman, Carole P. *Spies, Code Breakers, and Secret Agents: A World War II Book for Kids.* Emeryville, CA: Rockridge Press, 2019.

Ruelle, Karen Gray. *Surprising Spies: Unexpected Heroes of World War II.* New York: Holiday House, 2020.

INTERNET SITES

DK FIndout!: French Resistance
dkfindout.com/uk/history/world-war-ii/french-Resistance

History for Kids: World War II Facts for Kids
historyforkids.org/wwii

National Geographic Kids: 10 Facts about World War 2
natgeokids.com/uk/discover/history/general-history/world-war-two

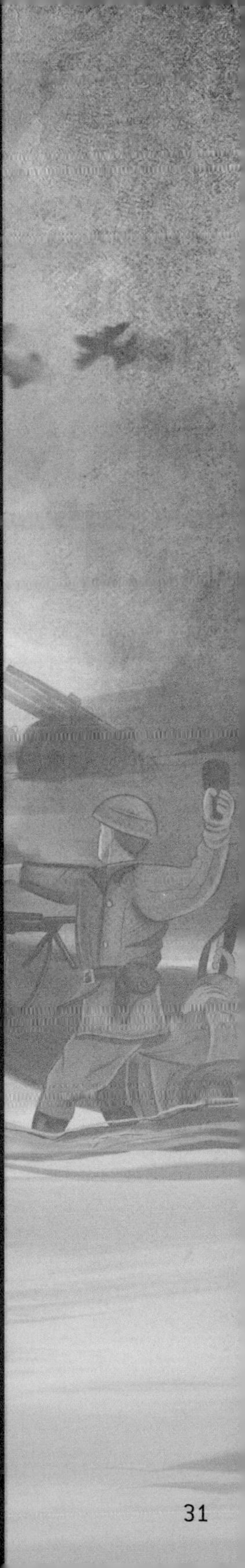

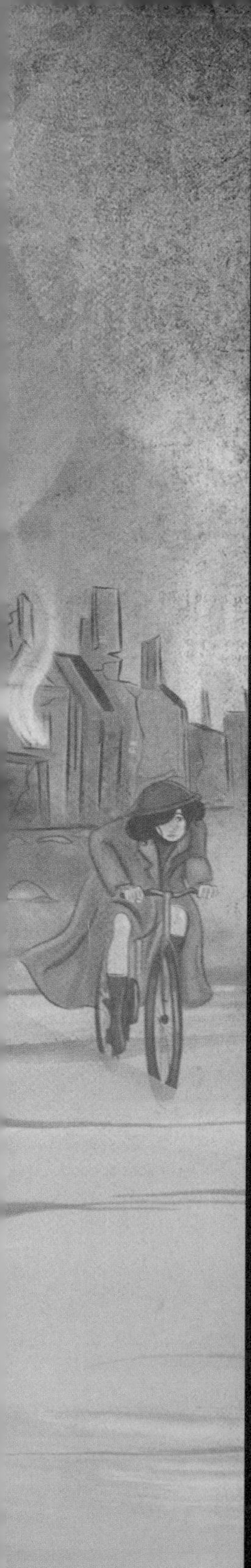

ABOUT THE AUTHOR

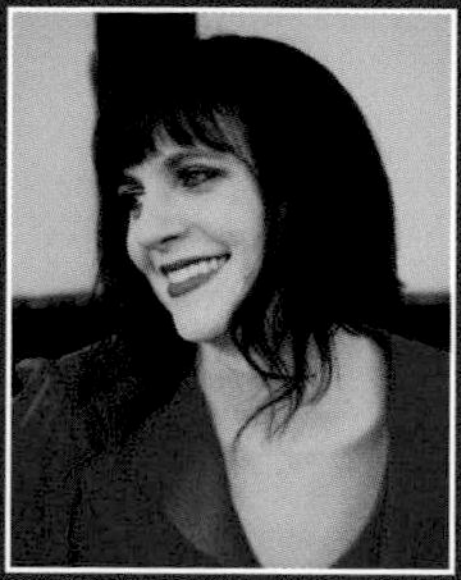

Jessica Gunderson grew up in the small town of Washburn, North Dakota. She has a bachelor's degree from the University of North Dakota and an MFA in Creative Writing from Minnesota State University, Mankato. She has written more than 50 books for young readers. Her book *Ropes of Revolution* won the 2008 Moonbeam Award for best graphic novel. She currently lives in Madison, Wisconsin, with her husband and cat.

ABOUT THE ILLUSTRATOR

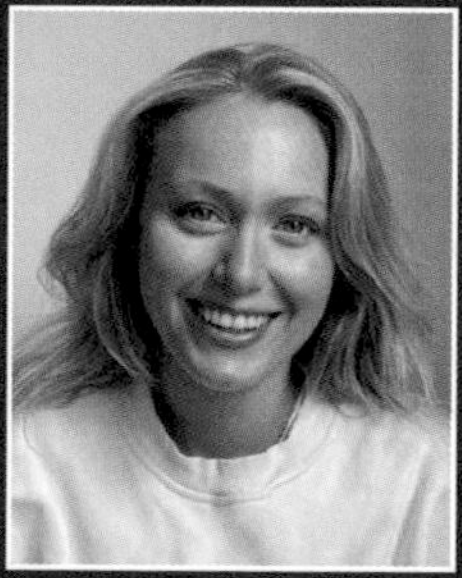

Alice Larsson is a London-based illustrator originally from Sweden. A natural creative, she is thrilled to be able to connect characters and stories through her work. Outside of drawing, Alice loves spending time with family and friends, as well as reading as many books as possible, which sparks her creativity. Alice has worked with a variety of publishers and writers on a wide range of international projects but focuses mainly on educational books and children's storybooks.